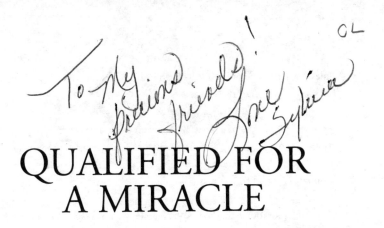

QUALIFIED FOR A MIRACLE

SECRETS TO RECEIVING FROM GOD

by Jim Hockaday

Jim Hockaday Ministries, Inc
Broken Arrow, Oklahoma

3496

05 04 03 02 01   10 9 8 7 6 5 4 3 2 1

Qualified for a Miracle:
Secrets to Receiving From God
ISBN 0-9767161-0-0
Copyright © 2002 by Jim Hockaday
P.O. Box 839
Broken Arrow, Oklahoma 74013

Published by Jim Hockaday Ministries, Inc.
P.O. Box 839
Broken Arrow, Oklahoma 74013

DEDICATION

This book is dedicated to those whose lives God ordained to influence my life.

Kenneth E. Hagin, Founder of Rhema Bible Training Center.

Kenneth Hagin, Jr., Pastor of Rhema Bible Church.

Dr. Doyle "Buddy" Harrison, Founder and President of FCF until November 28, 1998.

Each of these godly men greatly inspired me as they taught the Word, lived the Word, and personally exemplified the Life of God. God used them to encourage me as a young minister in my first years of teaching Prayer and Healing classes at Rhema Bible Training Center.

Pastor Buddy is the reason the teachings presented in this book are now in print. He was persuaded that others should take a look at faith from the other side of the mountain. So it is to those people who are "hungry" and in pursuit of their miracle that I also dedicate this book. To those who, perhaps, have tried all the other ways and not been successful, I write this book that they may "...taste and see that the Lord is good; blessed is the man that trusteth in Him" (Ps. 34:8).

CONTENTS

INTRODUCTION

I am so excited you've opened this book, because the revelation it contains is power to heal you and bring every promise God has made into your life. As you read, remember like Paul, I am writing not with "enticing words of man's wisdom, but in demonstration of the Spirit and of power: that your faith should not stand in the wisdom of men, but in the power of God" (1 Cor. 2:4,5). When you understand the significance of these words, God can touch you and manifest Himself with miracles in your life.

For too long, many Christians have been bound by feelings of intimidation and insufficiency in the area of faith. They reflect on their lives as Christians and remember past "faith failures." Then, when they are confronted with the biggest battles of their lives, their minds are convinced they cannot win.

This is exactly what the devil wants to happen. Moreover, it is exactly the opposite of what should happen in the life of a believer.

If you have received Christ as your Lord, then you are qualified to receive from God.

Not only did He qualify you, but He also provided a Book to explain what that means. The subject of faith is nothing new to the body of Christ. We cannot please God without faith. (Heb. 11:6.) That is why He has provided a mountain of truth about it in His Word.

There are many angles from which to view every mountain. The same is true in our approach to faith. If we spend our lives standing on one side of this mountain, then we are unable to benefit from the magnificent view of the truth in its entirety.

If the same Spirit who raised Christ from the grave dwells in you, then discover what He will do for you. Way's translation of Romans 8:11 says, "He'll thrill with new life your very bodies—those mortal bodies of yours—by the agency of His own Spirit, which now has its home in you."[1]

When Jesus took the ridicule, the curse, the sin, sickness, and disease of all mankind upon Himself, the Holy Spirit came in Him and raised Him out of the grave. The Holy Spirit will raise you just as He raised Jesus.

The Holy Spirit is a secret agent on assignment to rid your body of sickness and disease and establish God's will in every area of your life.

Jesus said in John 6:63, "My words are spirit and life." As you read His Words, remember they are full of the life of God. Set aside doubt today and believe His Word sets you free and brings the miracle you desire.

You are invited to a new perspective as a qualified believer. It can free you from the captivity of your limited ability. You cannot walk in the faith of God in your own power.

Reawaken your desire for the miracle that was too intimidating to pursue. Get hungry for it. Decide in your heart, *I'm absolutely not finishing this book without it* and watch what God can do when you discover how you are *Qualified for a Miracle!*

QUALIFIED FOR A MIRACLE

Chapter One

The Father of Faith

❧

And he believed in the Lord; and he counted it to him for righteousness (Genesis 15:6).

From Genesis 12-25, the story of the trusting relationship between God and Abraham unfolds. Though Abraham lived thousands of years ago, his story still helps us more fully understand and appreciate God and what He has done for us.

In Genesis 15:1, God told Abram, whom God would later rename Abraham, "Fear not, Abram: I am thy shield, and thy exceeding great reward." God's covenant with Abram said "My shield is now your shield, and My reward is now your reward." God came into covenant with Abram and exchanged His ability for Abram's ability.

Verses 2-3 show Abram's response:

Lord God, what wilt thou give me, seeing I go childless, and the steward of my house is this Eliezer of Damascus? And Abram said, Behold, to me thou hast given no seed: and, lo, one born in my house is mine heir.

> *God made it simple for Abram to act on His Word.*

Abram's response was a question. Abram said, "What are You going to give me, seeing that I go childless? The only heir I have is Eliezer of Damascus."

Notice, God didn't have any problem with Abram asking the question. He simply responded, saying, "This shall not be thine heir; but he that shall come forth out of thine own bowels shall be thine heir" (Gen. 15:4). God essentially said, "No, that boy will not be your heir, but one who will come from your own body and Sarah's body will be your heir."

Notice what the Lord did next.

And he brought him forth abroad, and said, Look now toward heaven, and tell the stars, if thou be able to number them: and he said unto him, So shall thy seed be (Genesis 15:5).

God said, "Walk outside, look at the stars and see if you're able to count them. So shall your seed be: You will not be able to count them."

It was not difficult for Abram to obey God by simply looking at the stars. Can you see how easy that was? God made it simple for Abram to act on His Word.

God keeps it simple. When God establishes any law for His people, He does it on our level—not His—because His level is beyond our comprehension.

Consider this example. Would it be reasonable to think I would give my six-year old child a calculus problem that I had difficulty solving myself?

Wouldn't it be ridiculous if I then said, "Contingent upon your completion of this problem, I will bless you"? That would be a ridiculous expectation; she barely knows how to subtract.

So, what am I going to do with my child?

Well, she does know how to count, so I will say, "Honey, how many apples do I have?"

"One, *two.*"

God's objective is to bless all who believe Him.

"All right; what happens if I take one apple away? How many do I have? Count that."

"One."

"That's right. Guess what, honey."

"What?"

"You get blessed." Then I give her something.

Do you know what she will want to do again?

Of course, she'll soon be saying, "Daddy, can I play the apple game again?" She will learn the system quickly.

Now think about this. You are God's child, and God knows you are a quick learner too. Blessing you is one of the greatest joys of God's heart. He simplified the system for you to receive His blessing.

FAITH ACTS ON GOD'S WORD

God's system is faith. God established the simple law of faith for Abram like this: God would move on Abram's behalf when Abram put his faith in God.

This was the system God designed to bless all of His people while they were on earth. His objective was, is, and will always be, to bless all who believe Him.

Therefore, when Abram asked, "What are You going to give me, seeing that I go childless?" God responded on the simplest level possible.

God was preparing Abram so that when it came time to take a leap of faith, when normally a person would not, Abram would. That is why God answered Abram by saying, simply, "Go outside and look at the stars."

Abram could most certainly do that! He went outside and looked at the stars, which God told him represented his kids.

Do you know why God asked Abram to do this? He was using an illustration from the natural realm to help validate Abram's belief. God was assuring Abram of what He knew he would have.

Can you see how simple it was for Abram to respond in obedience to God? It was no more difficult for Abram to respond than it is for a toddler to say, "Daddy...."

My kids would wear me out if I set up that system. Yet God wants His people to be able to approach Him in faith and say, "Daddy..." so that He can bless us with what we need for that very moment.

It's true, God is blessed when we are blessed because the fruit that we produce by believing Him always goes back to Him as people glorify the great, awesome, and mighty God. Everyone around us will see that we have learned how to cooperate with God and that supernatural things are always happening in our lives. Then we get to tell them about Jesus.

Then when they say, "Well, I'd like to have a relationship like that with a God who loves me," we can introduce them to our heavenly Father.

This is what will cause the rest of the world to want God: seeing our faith—our natural ability to believe and to be blessed. When we learn how to do what we are supposed to do, God not only blesses us, but His blessings open the whole world to our witness. This is all part of God's divine system of faith.

If faith is the system God designed through which to bless us, then He will work with us at our level so He can help us take a step of faith. The way He worked with Abram was to tell him, "Look at the stars."

When Abram obeyed God and gazed at those millions of glittering lights, he was so convinced of God's promise of his son and his son's sons and the ultimate Son—the Christ—and the multitude of sons who would come through Christ, that he was satisfied and believed. Genesis 15:6 says, "He believed in the Lord; and [God] counted it to him for righteousness."

GOD WAS MOVING ABRAM
INTO UNWAVERING BELIEF

Now look at the next verse: And "he said unto him, I am the Lord that brought thee out of Ur of the Chaldees, to give thee this land to inherit it" (v. 7).

God viewed Abram's question as worthy of an answer.

God wanted to move Abram into the place of unwavering belief in Him. In fact, God's ultimate desire for all His children is to move us into that place of unwavering belief in Him. When God manifests what we believe, it brings glory to Him, blessing to humanity, and souls into the kingdom of God as a sign and a wonder.

However, Abram was just beginning to learn to trust God. So when God gave Abram the promise that he would possess this huge expanse of land, Abram responded with a question: "Lord God, whereby shall I know that I shall inherit it?"(v. 8).

Again, Abram questioned God, but this didn't bother God. He viewed Abram's question as worthy of an answer.

God gave Abram a reply because He knew Abram's knowledge was the key to God's ultimate desire for Abram to believe in Him. He knew Abram could only participate effectively in what he knew.

So in answer to Abram's question, God said, "Take me an heifer of three years old, and a she goat of three years old, and a ram of three years old, and a turtledove, and a young pigeon" (v. 9).

You may be thinking *What kind of answer is that? 'Bring me a three-year old heifer, a three-year old goat, a three-year-old ram, a turtledove, and a pigeon'?*

ABRAM'S THOROUGH RESPONSE

Abram needed that exact answer. Let me show you why. Verse 10 shows us Abram's response: "And he took unto him all these, and divided them in the midst, and laid each piece one against another: but the birds divided he not." Abram brought all of these animals to God and cut them in two, down the middle, and placed each piece opposite the other; but he did not cut the birds in two.

Let me help you see the significance of Abram's response. What, specifically, did God ask Abram to do in verse 9? As you recall, God said, "Take me an heifer of three years old, and a she goat of three years old, and a ram of three years old, and a turtledove, and a young pigeon." That was the end of God's instruction.

Then verse 10 shows us how Abram responded to God's direction: "And he took unto him all these...." It seems that in this first phrase Abram completed what God had asked him to do. However, within that same verse, we see Abram continuing to do something: "...and divided them in the midst, and laid each piece one against another: but the birds divided he not."

If Abram had only been doing what God said, then verse 10 would only say, "And he took unto him all these."

Why is there something else? Why is there such specific detail about what Abram did in response to God's instruction? Verse 10 says that Abram brought these to Him *and* cut them in two. Then it tells us how he did it: down the middle. *He* placed each piece opposite the other. Then notice the last part of the verse: "but the birds divided he not."

Why didn't he divide the birds? Obviously, Abram had a reason for leaving the birds intact though he had divided all the others.

Apparently God's request was something Abram had already known. Not only could Abram fulfill God's initial command, but he could also perform these other functions without God even telling him to.

To strengthen our comprehension of the position that God has taken toward Abram, let's briefly discuss the covenant ceremony. Abram prepared the animals for the ceremony and even had to defend his preparation when the fowls came down upon the carcasses to defile it. (Gen. 15:11).

> *In order for God to cut a covenant He had to find someone equal to or greater than Himself.*

Now Abram was a fervent man, yet God still could not use him to participate in the covenant ceremony. Had Abram participated it would have been similar to you or I working for our salvation. Remember, believing in what God has done, and applying our faith is the way we receive from God.

In order for God to cut a covenant He had to find someone equal to or greater than Himself. Hebrews 6:12 says, "…because God could find no one greater, He cut the covenant with Himself." Genesis 15:12 says that Abram fell into a deep sleep or darkness. This means God "removed" Abram from the actual ceremony but in view of it. Abram could see what was taking place, and he described it in verse 17 as "...a smoking furnace, and a burning torch passed between those pieces." In other words what Abram witnessed was God Himself—Father and Son—in their brightness and glory cutting the covenant on behalf of Abram.

The same thing took place a few thousand years later when the whole world witnessed Jesus hanging on the cross. He was doing a work on our behalf that we could not do ourselves—the surety and fulfillment of our covenant. Like Abram, the only thing necessary for us to do to have our names included in the covenant is to *believe*. This Abram did—and so have we!

Ancient civilization shows evidence that the blood covenant was held in high esteem. It was used as the most solemn pact between two parties for absolute trust and reliability. The symbol of the blood covenant was first seen in the Garden of Eden in Genesis 3:21 when God shed the blood of an animal to provide a covering for man's shame.

This covenant progressed into the most legal contract that man owned.

So the blood covenant was a part of Abram's upbringing; it wasn't something completely new and foreign to him. God had been training him. This was part of the reason Abram knew God would do what He had said.

Do you see the heart of God in this? He didn't just want to get this wonderful blessing of land and children to Abram; He wanted to help Abram grow and develop spiritually and follow Him at His command. Therefore, He taught Abram on Abram's level.

The natural things that God did on Abram's level helped him trust and instantly believe what God said.

When Abram asked in verse 8, "Lord, how do I know that I'll inherit the land?" What if God had said, "Well, you'll know when you can figure out Einstein's law of relativity"?

Abram would have said, "Who's Einstein?" Einstein was 6000 years away! Abram would have been defeated. That would have created within Abram indecisiveness, insecurity, and intimidation—the antitheses of faith.

ABRAHAM'S GREAT TRUST

Abram was going to have to step out and believe God so much that he would put his son Isaac—who God promised would father a multitude of people—on an altar, believing God would most certainly raise him from the dead.

The natural things that God did on Abram's level helped him trust and instantly believe what God said, regardless of how impossible it seemed. Because of this early training, regardless of what God said, Abram's reply would be "If God said it, I'm doing it."

Indeed, the Bible shows us that when God said, "Take your son and sacrifice him on the altar," Abraham got the wood, prepared the donkey, and said, "Come on, son, let's go."

Unlike what many of us would do in his place, Abraham didn't even consider asking, "Do what? What do You want me to do with my son? Take him on a journey? Did You say *sacrifice?* Did You say, 'Put him on an altar'? Did You say, 'Kill him'? Remember, Lord, You said this is the one through whom all the nations of the earth shall be blessed."

No, Abraham simply obeyed. He believed that whatever God said would happen, would happen. He decided, *If God wants to do this to test my faith, that's fine. I trust Him so much that I'll do whatever He says. If I put a knife to my son's throat and kill him on the altar, I will watch him come back to life. God will have to do it, or I will bring His Word right to His face and say, "You have violated Your covenant."*

Do you realize the degree of trust that Abraham must have had in God? Where did he learn it? He learned it from God, who had worked with him and had instructed him in believing. God had helped Abraham develop such trust that he was eventually able to do whatever God asked of him, without question. And because of Abraham's faith,

God was able to bless multitudes of people, including you and me.

Now I want you to think about something. If Abraham lived under the old covenant and yet believed God to the degree that he would do anything God told him to do, then what does that mean for us who live in a new and better covenant?

Chapter Two

Living in a
New Covenant

❧

But now hath he obtained a more excellent
ministry, by how much also he is the media-
tor of a better covenant, which was established
upon better promises (Hebrews 8:6).

We live under a new and better covenant than did our
father of faith, Abraham. Our spirits encapsulate God's

very nature, and yet many of us are afraid to demonstrate our faith.

> *Jesus became as we are, so that we could become as He is.*

For instance, many Christians are afraid to step out and believe that God can mend their relationships, heal their bodies, or provide for their needs.

We have lost the integrity of real belief. In this present disrespectful, dishonest and dishonorable world, the devil is working hard to destroy the Christian's belief in a God who is able to deliver us from the mouths of lions (Dan. 6:16-23) and from the fires of furnaces. (Dan. 3:19-27.)

God cut a blood covenant with Abram to establish the absoluteness of His desire and willingness to bless him. Abraham dared to do the unthinkable, step out, and believe God. And God, who had bound Himself in a covenant with him, came to his side to protect him.

Sadly, today even we Christians don't know very much about covenants. Because of the lack of integrity constantly displayed around us, we have subconsciously diminished the meaning of *covenant* to a legal document we sign and have three days to call off.

So now, many of us don't even have an inkling of what God's covenant is. Consequently, even if we don't say it aloud, many may think this life of faith is difficult. With such a stalwart example in Abraham, as a man of faith, how could God make things any better? The New Testament shares this great quest and its accomplishment.

About 2000 years ago, there was a great exchange between God and man. Jesus Christ came to earth as the Son of Man, so that we might become sons of God. Jesus became as we are, so that we could become as He is. (1 John 4:17.) He went to hell, where we were to go, so that we could go to heaven, where He came from. (Heb. 2:14-16; Rev. 1:18.)

Did you know that Jesus became sin? Second Corinthians 5:21 says, "For he (God) hath made him to be sin for us, who knew no sin; that we might be made the righteousness of God in him." You see, when Jesus sweat great drops of blood in the Garden of Gethsemane (Luke 22:44), it wasn't only because He dreaded being physically nailed to a cross. The thing He loathed was knowing that He would be separated from almighty God—that He would become sin. He would become the sacrifice that would reconcile the world to God.

When Christ hung on the cross, He became your sin and my sin. When He cried out, "My God! My God! Why have You forsaken Me?" (Mark 15:34) it was because God had turned His back upon the sin that His Son had just become. God could not then, nor will He ever be able to, fellowship with sin.

The moment Jesus gave up His spirit and died for you and me, the veil was rent (Matt. 27:51), and the presence of God came out of the old tabernacle and the Ark of the Covenant. In three days God would make His dwelling place the heart of man.

Jesus, who embodied the sins of the entire world, went to a place of torment. He suffered for three days and three nights in hell, where we would have to go were it not for this great exchange.

Exchange is what covenant is all about. The divine exchange of the new covenant is no small thing. It is marked with the potency of the redemption that we have in Christ Jesus—the redemption that gives us mastery over sin, sickness, disease, and every other thing from the kingdom of darkness.

YOU BECAME A BELIEVER

When you received Jesus Christ as your Lord and Savior, God came into covenant with you: He exchanged your life and nature for His life and nature. He immediately made you a brand new creature. (2 Cor. 5:17.) *You became what is called a believer.*

Although Abraham was called "believing Abraham" in Galatians

God's ultimate goal for Abraham, and indeed all of humankind, was to get him to believe.

3:9, He was not a *believer* in the same sense that you and I are. He was not born again. Believing was what Abraham did; it was not who he was. God's ultimate goal for Abraham, and indeed all of humankind, was to get him to believe.

God fulfilled this goal under the new covenant by creating us as believers. There was never a race of believers before the Cross; it was not until this side of the Cross. Now when a person is born again, he automatically becomes a believer. Within his nature is the ability of God to believe for anything. He steps into God's class with God's mountain-moving, unmatched divine nature. Automatically he has an advantage in life. Not only is God in him, but he is now capable of manifesting the power of God as easily as Jesus did on the earth.

God calls people who are born again "righteousness."

The living God, the very life of God, comes to dwell in us the moment we become born again. At that moment, we become believers by nature. We have a new tag to our name: "believer."

The spirit of a man or a woman is either a believer or an unbeliever. As believers, we need to know that our spirits do not contain even one ounce of doubt or unbelief. We are believers by nature.

A believer simply cannot doubt. It is impossible. The only thing a believer can do is believe. That is because he contains God's nature—the divine ability of God to believe for anything.

If God designed us with His nature, then we should know what the divine nature of God looks like. In 2 Corinthians 6:14 Paul shows us by differentiating between someone who has God's divine nature and someone who does not: "Be ye not unequally yoked together with unbelievers: for what fellowship hath right-eousness with unrighteousness? and what communion hath light with darkness?"

So through the apostle Paul, God calls people who are born again "righteousness." Now, religion may never call you righteousness, but God does. Perhaps some traditional teaching has made you feel less than righteous and has led you to believe that if you weren't such an undeserving person, you could become righteous, and then maybe your prayers would avail much.

A preacher may have spent a lot of time preaching about how you are supposed to dress or wear your hair to appear externally righteous. But God said if you're born again, you're righteous; and if not, you're unrighteous.

A NEW PRODUCT CALLED LIGHT

"What fellowship has light with darkness?" Paul continued in 2 Corinthians 6:14. So he called people who are born again *light,* and people who have a sin nature He called *darkness.*

Throughout the Word, darkness represents the devil's kingdom. For example, 1 John 1:5 says, "God is light, and in him is no darkness at all."

What is the byproduct of people's sin nature? Their minds and their flesh are touched by their sin nature. Their inner selves affect their minds and their bodies, until it is natural for them to do the works of the devil, or the works of darkness. They continually manifest the darkness within them.

On the other end of the spectrum, the light inside us should touch our minds and our bodies. John 1:4 says, "In him was life; and the life was the light of men." We should continually manifest the works of light because Christ, the light, is in us. First John 1:5 says, "God is light, and in him is no darkness at all." Therefore, we should never manifest the works of darkness.

If the effect of a sin-natured spirit is a perverted mind and a body that sins, then the effect of a divine-natured spirit is a mind that thinks the thoughts of God and a body that performs the actions of God. Indeed, 1 Corinthians 2:16 says that we now have the mind of Christ.

First John 3:9 shows us the result of Christ's nature in us: "Whosoever is born of God doth not commit sin; for his seed remaineth in him: and he cannot sin, because he is born of God." In other words, he said, "If you're of God, you don't sin. You don't practice sin, because you have a new nature. You might mess up once in a while, but you don't practice sin."

If the light of God is in us, then the darkness of sin will not lurk in our hearts. Paul asked, "What communion hath light with darkness?" (2 Cor. 6:14). If our new nature is light, then no darkness at all can dwell in us.

> *Just as brides traditionally take on the names of their husbands, when we become Christians we take on the name of Christ.*

Now notice what Paul said in verse 15: "And what concord hath Christ with Belial?" Paul, inspired by the Holy Spirit, called the church "Christ." Some people in the church would like to hang a person for saying this, yet Paul called the church Christ and you and I are members.

If Christ is the Head and we are the body, then what are we going to call ourselves? Your head and your body go by the same name. Then it makes sense that Paul calls Christ's body the same name he calls the Head.

Paul says in 2 Corinthians 6:14-15 that because we are born again, we are light, we are righteousness, and we are Christ. Now, we know there is one Jesus Christ, but there are many heirs with Christ. (Rom. 8:17.)

Christ means "the anointed One and His anointing." And according to 1 John 2:27, when Jesus is our Lord, His anointing resides in us:

> But the anointing which ye have received of him abideth in you, and ye need not that any man teach you: but as the same anointing teacheth you of all things, and is truth, and is no lie, and even as it hath taught you, ye shall abide in him.

Just as brides traditionally take on the names of their husbands, when we become Christians we take on the name of Christ. There is only one Jesus Christ, but there's a Jane Christ, a John Christ, and so forth. We simply call them Christians.

That name comes with His anointing. When we say, "I'm a Christian," we are really saying, "I am an anointed one with Jesus' anointing."

How did we get that way? We have His nature. Nothing of ourselves is left in us. Our nature is no longer "natural" in human terms; it's supernatural.

We have to see ourselves changed! We are no longer just human-natured.

YOU HAVE BECOME LIKE GOD

When you are born again, what are you inside? I'm not asking what you're trying to be, what you think you will be if you've heard enough or studied enough, or what you are when you feel adequate enough or when the pressures of life are not there. I'm asking, "What are you the very moment that you become born again?"

The reason this is difficult is that before we were born again, we always thought of human beings with only a will, intellect, emotion, and body. You possess the same "stuff" or materiality that God has in Him—the same life, nature, ability, and anointing.

Just for the sake of illustration, I want you to imagine something. What would you do if God said, "I'm going to do something I've never done before: I'm going to doubt."

You would laugh and say, "No way, Lord! You can't do that. That is not Your nature; You don't even have any doubt in You. Your Word says, 'In Him is light and no darkness at all.'"

If you, a believer, said, "I'm going to doubt," I'd say, "No you're not. You can't. It's impossible."

You might say, "I'm just going to go by my head and all the senses of the world and see what my body has to say, and that's how I'm going to live."

Doubt is unnatural.

That you *can* do. As you recall, Romans 1:26-27 tells us of people going against their nature. They opposed what was natural and persisted in their pursuit of their unnatural desires, until God gave them over to a debased mind. (v. 28.) In other words, they continued down the wrong road until that wrong road became natural for them.

That is what many Christians do. They live out of the unnatural realm of the senses and the flesh, which have been subject to the old nature for a long time. They are unaware that they are new, divine-natured beings, filled with God's ability. They don't realize they are believers, whose faith can never fail. Doubt is unnatural.

The dilemma is not whether or not we are *able* to believe; it is whether or not we allow our believing spirits to rule.

Our brains and bodies were always in cahoots. When our bodies felt ill, our minds told us to call the doctor, and we did. When our taste buds wanted a milkshake, our mind told us to get one—whether we needed it or not—and we did. When our emotions were moved to just yell at our spouses, children, or colleagues and tell them what we thought, we did it. We did exactly what our mind and body *felt* like doing.

Therefore, when we became born again, our minds and bodies thought they were still in control. They didn't know that in truth our spirits had become mighty. We had become *believers.*

Do you know what it means to be a believer by nature? Jesus, our great example, was the first man on earth since Adam who was a believer by nature. Did you ever see Jesus full of anxiety and worry? No, Jesus was in control all the time.

Did you ever see Jesus saying, "Oh, a demon! I need to go pray a little bit and get built up"? No, with confidence He walked up to a demon and said, "Come out!"

Was Jesus afraid when the sea was raging? Did He say, "We're going to sink"? No. He had already said, "We're going to the other side." (Mark 4:35.) How did He know that? He knew that the storm could not stop them, because, while spending time with His Father, He had already seen the ship on the other side.

A sea couldn't stop Him. Nothing in this world had anything on Him. He had a divine commission and a divine plan. He was unscathed by sin, so He was free from condemnation. He never felt the grip of inferiority or intimidation.

In His mind, if a sea was raging, that just meant He had an opportunity to tell it to stop. So this is what He did:

He arose, and rebuked the wind, and said unto the sea, Peace, be still. And the wind ceased, and there was a great calm (Mark 4:39).

And the astonished disciples stepped back in the boat and said, "What kind of man is this?" (Mark 4:41.)

He was a believer!

Anything God promises will be easy for us to believe and receive.

WHAT KIND OF MAN OR WOMAN ARE YOU?

What kind of man or woman are you? The Man who sent demons fleeing and stilled the sea lives inside of you. You have His very nature. You are a believer. That is who you are.

If you stepped out in the faith of God that resides within you, you would startle many Christians. They wouldn't know what to think of you. They would ask, "What kind of person is this?"

YOU ARE A BELIEVER

What do runners do best? They run. So, what do believers do best? We believe!

That means if we will submit our head and our body to our "heart," ultimately our real self, our entire being will believe. And that means anything God promises will be easy for us to believe and receive.

Thinking it is natural for a believer to doubt would be as ridiculous as thinking it is natural for a dog to climb trees, drink milk, use a litter box, and scratch furniture. Believers believe!

This is a very simple truth, but can you see the validity of it? If you begin to meditate on this thought, you will realize *that your miracle is waiting for you!*

He made it this simple: It's easy for you to believe, because believing is what believers do best!

BELIEVING IS CALLED FAITH

As a believer, the only thing you need to do is to respond to Him with the action of believing. Your simple believing response to God's promise is called faith; and as a believer, responding in faith is the most natural thing you can do.

As a Christian, you should be excited about believing. You should be saying, "You mean the system is faith, Lord? You mean all I have to do is believe? That is too easy! That is what I do; that's who I am! I am a believer! Surely there's more to it."

Remember God worked with Abraham to produce strong, effective faith. However, Abraham was not born again. The *new and improved plan* was to recreate man's spirit until, by nature, he would always succeed—for he had become a "believer!"

Chapter Three

The Divine Nature

❦

For by grace are ye saved through faith; and that not of yourselves: it is the gift of God: not of works, lest any man should boast. For we are his workmanship, created in Christ Jesus unto good works, which God hath before ordained that we should walk in them? (Ephesians 2:8-10).

God made humanity in His image and in His likeness. Genesis 1:27 says, "God created man in his own image, in the image of God created he him; male and female created he them."

He gave them His nature. All people are born into this world with a nature that will cause them to respond naturally according to that nature.

The word *nature* means "origin; the sum of innate properties and powers by which one person differs from another; distinctive, native peculiarities; natural characteristics."[2]

Because of a person's nature, he has innate tendencies to do certain things. These innate properties and powers were not necessarily learned but were placed inside of him and were at work within him while he was developing.

This principle is even true in the animal kingdom. For example, a puppy doesn't have to be around other dogs to learn how to bark. If you separate a puppy from its mother the moment it is born, what will that puppy do in a few days? It will bark. Why? That's its nature. You don't have to teach it by surrounding it with other dogs. Now, you could train that dog to bark more often or to bark on command, but you don't have to teach it *how* to bark.

Likewise, if a person has a sin nature, he doesn't have to learn how to sin; it just comes naturally. If he spends time with other sin-natured people, he may learn how to sin a whole lot more than he would have if he hadn't had other people showing him how to do it. However, if a person has a sin nature, then he will have certain innate tendencies.

SPIRITUAL NATURE AFFECTS BODY AND MIND

We can see that in Ephesians 2:1-3 NIV:

As for you, you were dead in your transgressions and sins, in which you used to live when you followed the ways of this world and of the ruler of the kingdom of the air, the spirit who is now at work in those who are disobedient. All of us also lived among them at one time, gratifying the cravings of our sinful nature and following its desires

> *Two areas of your life that a sin nature affects are your flesh and your mind.*

and thoughts. Like the rest, we were by nature objects of wrath.

Notice the two areas that the sin nature affects. Ephesians 2:3 in the *King James Version* says: "We all had our conversation in times past in the lusts of our flesh, fulfilling the desires of the flesh and of the mind...."

Therefore, the two areas of your life that a sin nature affects are your flesh and your mind.

Is a sin nature in the mind or in the flesh? No, a sin nature dwells in the *spirit* of a man or woman. The spirits of sin-natured men and women affect their minds and bodies so much that they are plagued until the works of sin naturally come.

Why doesn't it surprise us when we hear all the horrible things that are going on in the world? It is because we know sinners sin. It's nice to find a sinner who doesn't, but this doesn't grant him salvation. Ephesians 2:4-10 tells us how a person with a sin nature can gain salvation and an eternity in heaven:

But God, who is rich in mercy, for his great love wherewith he loved us, even when we were dead in sins, hath quickened us together with Christ, (by grace ye are saved;) and hath raised us up together, and made us sit together in heavenly places in Christ Jesus: that in the ages to come he might shew the exceeding riches of his grace in his kindness toward us through Christ Jesus. For by grace are ye saved through faith; and that not of yourselves: it is the gift of God: not of works, lest any man should boast. For we are his workmanship, created in Christ Jesus unto good works, which God hath before ordained that we should walk in them (Ephesians 2:4-10).

Only by God's grace does a sin-natured person receive God's nature. The nature of God becomes his nature; his innate tendencies are no longer toward sin but toward righteousness and all of God's attributes.

> *We are God's product, God's display, and God's work of art.*

41

As born-again believers, we no longer even have an old sin nature. We couldn't find it even if we wanted to. We no longer exist as sinners. We are *not* "sinners saved by grace," as traditional thinking suggests.

If we accept that kind of unbiblical thinking, then we will live beneath our means. Don't let that happen to you. God raised you up to sit together in heavenly places with Him. (Eph. 2:6.) He obviously sees someone of great importance when He sees you.

Notice verse 10 says, "We are his workmanship, created in Christ Jesus unto good works." *Workmanship* is a product that has been made.[3] *Create* means "to form; to shape; to completely change or transform."[4] We are God's product, God's display, and God's work of art. God created, formed, and fashioned us into a new being.

A NEW WINESKIN

God's relationship with humanity began when He breathed into Adam's nostrils and life entered the spirit, soul, and body of man causing that man to become a living being who began to function and move. Everything about Adam began to work according to God's design.

Today, God wants to reside inside His precious earthen vessels. He wants us to live a higher life, inhabited by Him, the unspeakably tremendous treasure. However, God cannot simply take residence in an unregenerate being. Jesus said:

> Neither do men put new wine into old [wineskins]: else the [wineskins] break, and the wine runneth out, and the [wineskins] perish: but they put new wine into new [wineskins], and both are preserved (Matthew 9:17).

This natural concept is very easily understood: New wine should not be poured into old wineskins, because new wine will burst an old wineskin. An old wineskin is brittle and cannot move with the contents. It does not expand very well.

This is exactly what we see in salvation. A person's unsaved spirit is like that old wineskin, and God is like that new wine. He cannot be inside of an old wineskin called a sin nature, because it is dry, brittle, and cracked. If God, or the new wine, were to get inside of an unsaved spirit—an old wineskin—that wineskin would absolutely burst and the new wine would be spilled.

Therefore, the human spirit needs to become a completely new substance, a new container, rubbed down with fresh oil by the Holy Spirit so that God can fill it.

God's divine nature is the new wineskin that our spirits become when they are reborn. Nothing can hold God but God. Therefore, this is how God fulfilled His purpose to dwell within us to bless us.

> *In order to preserve our spirits when His holy presence came inside, God lined our spirits with Himself.*

That purpose included preserving our spirits. Remember Jesus said, "Neither do men put new wine into old wineskins: else the wineskins break, and the wine runneth out, and the wineskins perish: but they put new wine into new wineskins, and both are preserved." When the skin is new, both the skin and the wine are preserved.

First Thessalonians 5:23 says, "And the very God of peace sanctify you wholly; and I pray God your whole spirit and soul and body be preserved blameless unto the coming of our Lord Jesus Christ." God wants to preserve your spirit, soul, and body. According to Strong's, that means God wants "to attend to carefully, "take care of," "guard," and "keep" your spirit, soul, and body.[1]

In order to preserve our spirits when His holy presence came inside, God lined our spirits with Himself.

Second Corinthians 5:17 tells us how the human spirit becomes a new container: "Therefore if any man be in Christ, he is a new creature [a new container]: old things are passed away; behold, all things are become new." *The Bible in Basic English*[2] translates it this way: "So if any man is in Christ, he is in a new world: the old things have come to an end; they have truly become new."

> *We're not trying to become like Jesus; we already are like Jesus!*

When a person becomes born again, he steps out of the old and into something completely new. Paul said in 2 Corinthians 5:17 that a believer has stepped into a new world. Jesus said that he has stepped into life:

> Most assuredly, I say to you, he who hears My word and believes in Him who sent Me has everlasting life, and shall not come into judgment, but has passed from death into life (John 5:24 NKJV).

However, some of us don't realize we've stepped from death into life and from one world into another. Though our bodies still touch this world, we are not supposed to live by its standards. Instead, we are to live by the standards of the new world, just as Jesus did.

The secret to Jesus' success was that as a man He walked in this earthly domain but lived by the rules, laws, and standards of the heavenly domain. On earth He exercised the laws of the heavenly world—laws like faith, love, mercy, and peace. (See John 3:13.)

I will let you in on a little secret: We're not trying to become like Jesus; we already are like Jesus!

Any man who is in Christ is in a new world order. As long as we are dominated by worldly thinking, we will live off the means of this world. But Christ Jesus elevated us when we became born again. Now that Christ is in control, we are living by the means of the new world.

WHAT HAPPENS TO THE OLD WINESKIN?

Romans 6:1-6 shows us what happens to the old sin nature when a person becomes born again.

What shall we say then? Shall we continue in sin, that grace may abound? God forbid. How shall we, that are dead to sin, live any longer therein?

Know ye not, that so many of us as were baptized into Jesus Christ were baptized into his death? Therefore we are buried with him by baptism into death: that like as Christ was raised up from the dead by the glory of the Father, even so we also should walk in newness of life.

For if we have been planted together in the likeness of his death, we shall be also in the likeness of his resurrection: knowing this, that our old man is crucified with him, that the body of sin might be destroyed, that henceforth we should not serve sin.

The moment a person confesses Jesus Christ as Savior, his old man is destroyed. His old container, or wineskin, is nailed to the cross with Christ and is completely annihilated.

Our "old man" can't get up any time he wants to. We don't have to keep working to put him down. Neither was our old man merely laid in a coffin with the lid nailed shut and then buried six feet under.

No, if you look up the terms *crucified with* and *buried with* in the original language, they denote a complete annihilation of the old self. *Strong's Concordance* says that if you are crucified with Christ, then you "have become utterly estranged from (dead to) [your] former habit of feeling and action."[3] It also says, "the former sinfulness is...utterly taken away."[4]

Therefore, when we became born again, our old wine-skins were destroyed. You are not your "old self" because God removed all evidence of our old sin natures from the record of all eternity. We do not have old natures.

You are not a refurbished, *old* creature. Second Corinthians 5:17 says, "If any man be in Christ, he is a *new* creature: old things are passed away; behold, all things are become new."

It says, *"All* things are new!" Our lives are brand new. Our spirits are entirely new creations, new works of art, crafted by Almighty God. And God doesn't make any failures.

This verse doesn't tell us how many old things passed away. It just says "old things." You might think, *Well, I had about five or six old things, but I have about three or four left.*

> *You're not just natural anymore; you're supernatural.*

However this verse does specify how many things have become new: *All* things have become new. And if all things are new, all old things passed away.

49

You can't have everything becoming new and still have an old thing. All things have become new, and all old things have passed away.

Just think about that. Meditate on it. Start to see yourself in this light. You are not the same person you were before you became a born-again believer. You're not just natural anymore; you're *super*natural. There is a whole new quality of Being inside of you. You are not at all who you used to be.

I'm not talking about what you look like in the mirror. You still have the same natural hair and eyes. I am talking about who you are inside, which is what affects how you look and act on the outside.

HIS SPIRIT DWELLS IN YOU

Speaking through the apostle Paul, God said, "But if the Spirit of him that raised up Jesus from the dead dwell in you, he that raised up Christ from the dead shall also quicken your mortal bodies by his Spirit that dwelleth in you" (Rom. 8:11).

This is what Paul was trying to say to the Corinthian church: "Don't you know that your body is the temple of the Holy Spirit and that God dwells in you?" (1 Cor. 6:19.)

Second Corinthians 4:7 also tells us that God's Spirit dwells in us: "But we have this treasure in earthen vessels, that the excellency of the power may be of God, and not of us."

God had to make each of us a new creation because God's Spirit wants to dwell in our imperfect earthen vessels. (2 Cor. 5:17.) In order to understand this concept, consider the following illustration.

If you were going to create a clay pot, you would get your little wheel going, get a piece of wet clay, shape it into a pot with your hands and let it dry.

That would be one creation. You couldn't take the substance of that pot and reform it to make a new creation.

Instead, if you wanted to make a new creation, you would get a new lump of clay—a new substance, a new material. You would put it on the wheel and make a new vessel, a new creation.

We have to understand what God did when He made us new creations. He didn't take old lumps of clay and just make them better. He made brand new pots out of brand new lumps of clay. *All* things have become new. We are new formations.

When He made us brand new, inside we became something we never were before. We are believers. That doesn't just mean we are now qualified to enter heaven; it means much more than that. It means we are a new substance, a new species. We are different than we used to be. We are new creations.

This new creation that you now are is a divine-natured being. Second Peter 1:4 verifies this, calling you, the believer, and a "partaker of the divine nature."

What kind of measure of this divine nature did God give us? In John 10:10, Jesus tells us, "I've come to give you life and life *more abundantly.*"

He's given us such an abundance of His divine nature that to think and act as a man—to do something in the same way someone who is not born again would do it—the Apostle Paul says in I Corinthians 3:3 would be far short of our heavenly potential.

We are so radically different from unsaved people that God calls us "light" and them "darkness." (2 Cor. 6:14.) We are completely distinct.

Through His Word, God is saying to us, I didn't just come to give you a little bit of life. I came to give you life in a great abundance far beyond what you'll ever need in this existence to do whatever I've told you to do.

It will get rid of every tumor; open the blind eye and the deaf ear; and the crippled leg will walk because of this material that is inside of you. And you can use it on a continual basis, because that nature is who you now are: I've made you a whole new being that looks and acts just like Me!

> *I've made you a whole new being that looks and acts just like Me!*

DADDY'S GENES

God didn't make any failures! As John 1:13 says, we're not born of the will of flesh, of the will of man or of blood; we're *born of God!*

I have certain natural traits because I have my father's genes. I make certain expressions that are just like my mom's. I walk and carry myself much the same as my dad does.

Now my oldest daughter is the "spitting image" of me. Not only in her appearance, but in her actions as well. She will stop a conversation to say, "Wait, wait, wait. Hey kids, listen now. This is what we're going to do." I watch her and think *where does she get this?* Then I am reminded—she has her daddy's genes.

Likewise, when my spirit became born again, I received my heavenly Daddy's genes. Glory to God, when I was born out of heaven, I received Jesus' genes. It's no wonder that I act, think, talk, and walk as He does: I have His genes! It's no wonder I cast out devils just as Jesus did: I have His genes! Hallelujah!

If we could just see who we are, we would be so certain that we are just like God that we would effortlessly start to manifest His nature.

In order for this to happen, though, our brains need some serious cleansing. I know mine is no exception. Not long ago I found myself verbalizing some traditional thinking I had grown up with. Someone asked me about a certain situation: "Well, how is it turning out?" And I replied, "Well, we'll just see what happens, and then we'll take the next step."

A Christian declares what is according to My Word, and then he watches it take place exactly as I said it.

The Lord got all over my case about that. He said, *I don't want you to ever say that again.*

I said, "Say what?" I had not even been conscious of what I said.

He said, *Don't ever say, "We're just going to see what happens." That is not the vocabulary of a Christian. A Christian declares what is according to My Word, and then he watches it take place exactly as I said it. You decide what you want and then you say it, and that is what will be. You will watch what you say come to pass. You're not going to "see what happens."*

Yes, Lord, I thought. I had been corrected, and since then I've been watching what I say come to pass instead of just "seeing what happens."

If we just "see what happens," we put ourselves over in the devil's hand, where he has room to operate and manipulate. Then we start thinking, *Well, I thought this was going to happen. But I guess we'll just have to go to plan B because apparently my faith is not working.*

No! It *will* work for a Christian. We're made in His image and in His likeness. When He speaks, He has what He says (Gen. 1:3); therefore, when we speak, we have what we say. (Mark 11:23.)

If we could just visualize the enormity of our God within us next to the puniness of sickness or any other problem, for that matter, then that image would dislodge our every fear. We would leave our beaten paths of doubt and change our direction of thought and action toward our divine nature within.

Paul prayed for the church, "until Christ be formed in her" (Gal. 4:19). Christ dwells in us, and through Him, we reflect the Father's image. As God's representatives on this earth, we are no longer just normal men and women who speak things that don't come to pass.

God is inside of us to such a degree that we are no longer just humans. We are sons and daughters of Almighty God. We are recipients of His very life and nature, and we have His ability to believe, which means it is impossible for our spirits to doubt. Let's discover why faith comes and why you are qualified to use it.

Chapter Four

God's Saving Faith

❧

B rethren, my heart's desire and prayer to God for Israel is, that they might be saved (Romans 10:1).

The great apostle Paul wrote, "My heart's desire and prayer for Israel is for their salvation." This is Paul's intro-duction to Romans Chapter 10, which is completely devoted to the topic of *salvation*. Throughout this chapter we will see the emphasis that Paul places on *faith*, how it comes to the sinner, and of its place in salvation.

Continuing in verse 2, Paul wrote, "For I bear them record that they have a zeal of God, but not according to knowledge." "These Israelites have a lot of zeal for God," Paul wrote. "They just don't know where to put their zeal. They're zealous to do works of righteousness according to the Law, but they don't realize God has already provided them with His righteousness through the Messiah."

Indeed, anyone who wanted to obey Jewish Law had to have zeal, because it contained very rigid regulations for every area of life. Paul addressed such individuals who were running after salvation as well as they possibly could according to these rules.

In verse 3, Paul continued, saying, "For they being ignorant of God's righteousness, and going about to establish their own righteousness, have not submitted themselves unto the righteousness of God." In other words, he was telling these individuals, "You need to know how to put your zeal in the right place so you can get the right result."

What they needed to understand was that when Jesus died, God's presence came out of the temple. Mark 15:38 says that the veil was rent. Now God's Spirit could come into a new temple, called a human spirit, to make His abode forever.

We must accept God's gift of righteousness.

Because they didn't understand this, they were still operating under the old Mosaic Law, doing the best they could to gain some kind of salvation. We know, according to Isaiah 64:6, that all of our works are as filthy rags.

Our own works of righteousness don't earn salvation. It is only because Jesus became sin that we can become the righteousness of God. (2 Cor. 5:21.) It is God's righteousness that makes us righteous.

Therefore, we must accept God's gift of righteousness. Romans 6:23 tells us, "For the wages of sin is death;

but the gift of God is eternal life through Jesus Christ our Lord."

Like these Jews, who were focused on their efforts to produce what God wanted in them, we also need to release what we're doing and trust Him to do it. He already knows what He can do best, and we already know what we can't do. So we ought to learn from this passage of Scripture and let God do His own work in our lives.

In Romans 10:4 Paul explained, "For Christ is the end of the law for righteousness to every one that believeth." In other words, when Christ arose, there was no more Law. If we walk by faith, then we don't need the Law. We will fulfill the Law in one law called the Law of love. (Gal. 5:14.)

In Romans 10:5-7 Paul continued to contrast the righteousness of the Law with God's gift of righteousness:

"For Moses describeth the righteousness which is of the law, That the man which doeth those things shall live by them. But the righteousness which is of faith speaketh on this wise, Say not in thine heart, Who shall ascend into heaven? (that is, to bring Christ down from above:) or, Who shall descend into the deep?" (That is, to bring up Christ again from the dead.)

In other words, Paul said, "Don't try to work out your righteousness as though you either have to go up to heaven and try to bring Christ down, or go down into the earth and try to bring Christ up."

GOD'S WORD IS HIS FAITH

Then in verse 8 he explained why such work is futile:

"But what saith it? The word is nigh thee, even in thy mouth, and in thy heart: that is, the word of faith, which we preach."

Paul was saying, "You already have faith because it's in the Word, which we've been preaching to you. Within that message is the faith for

God's belief is God's faith.

you to respond and to become born again. God believes His Word. He believes what He says and says what He believes. Thus, God's faith is His Word."

This is why God wants us to meditate on His Word: He wants us to understand how to use His faith. It's the same reason that I want my children to meditate on my words: I want them to know and operate in my beliefs.

For example, we have a swimming pool in our backyard, and my wife and I have taught our children they cannot go back there alone. Because we have instilled this belief in them, it has become their belief.

God wants to govern our lives with His beliefs for the same reason—to preserve and bless us. If we have His beliefs, then we can have His ways, because God's belief is God's faith.

When God gives us His belief in His Word, He's giving us His faith. This is what Paul was trying to show the Jewish people. They were zealous for God, but they were not walking in knowledge. They didn't realize that already within them was the ability to believe God.

Because Paul had preached to them, the Word of faith—or God's faith in the Word—had already come unto them, into their hearts. They didn't realize it, but they could call on the name of the Lord and be saved.

Paul knew that before his prayer for these Jews to be saved could be answered, they needed revelation. They were still ignorant of God's gift.

Ephesians 4:18 says that because of ignorance, people become alienated from the life of God. Indeed, if someone is ignorant of a certain biblical principle, he cannot act on it.

That is why these Jews needed to learn about the principle of faith. And that is why *we* need to learn about it. I am not talking about *our* faith; I am talking about the faith of God.

In order to understand the way God's faith works, consider this illustration. If a friend told me he would meet me at a certain place and at a certain time, then his promise would be his belief. Based on my friend's word, I would have my friend's faith, his belief.

Because I believe this friend to be honest, I would then act on that belief. I would be at the agreed-upon place at the agreed-upon time because he has given me his belief that he will be there.

Remember, I would be acting on my friend's faith. Many obstacles could prevent his arrival. His car could get a flat tire, for instance. So when the appointed time comes, he may not be there.

In that particular situation, can my faith—which is really *his* faith—make him appear? Obviously the answer is no. His faith is only as good as his ability to perform what he said he would do. If he told me he would meet me at three o'clock and it took him an extra half-hour to change the tire, then his faith could not make him meet me on time.

> *It doesn't come if you don't express what you believe.*

With that in mind, I want you to think about the faith of God. If this Word is, as Paul wrote, "the Word of faith"—in other words, if there is faith in this Word—then it comes with God's ability to do what it says when He says it will. Thus, knowing that all things are possible to him that believes (Mark 9:23) and that nothing is impossible with God (Luke 1:37), you can be sure that God's faith can back up what His Word says and make it *effective every time.*

That is what Paul wanted the people of Israel to understand. He said, "You have been hearing the Word of God—that is, the Word of faith—which we've preached to you. If you confess with your mouth the Lord Jesus and believe in your heart that God raised Him from the dead, then you will be saved." (Rom. 10:8,9.)

He was telling them, "You already have faith for salvation because you've heard us preach the Word, God's faith. Now speak it. It doesn't come if you don't express what you believe. It doesn't come by trying to fulfill all of the Mosaic Law. No, salvation comes by simply believing that Jesus Christ is Lord, that He died, and that He rose again and by confessing with your mouth Jesus as Lord."

For with the heart man believeth unto righteousness; and with the mouth confession is made unto salvation. For the scripture saith, Whosoever believeth on him shall not be ashamed. For there is no difference between the Jew and the Greek: for the same Lord over all is rich unto all that call upon him. For whosoever shall call upon the name of the Lord shall be saved (Romans 10:10-13).

Paul was saying, "All you need to do is believe in the Lord and call on His name, and you shall be saved. Don't try to become born again by the Law when you can be liberated by faith in God!"

THE STEPS TOWARD SALVATION

Then, in verse 14 and 15, Paul enumerated the steps that lead a person toward calling upon God for salvation.

How then shall they call on him in whom they have not believed? and how shall they believe in him of whom they have not heard? and how shall they hear without a preacher? And how shall they preach, except they be sent? (Romans 10:14,15).

First in the progression toward a person's receiving salvation, Paul wrote, someone sends a preacher. Second, the preacher preaches the gospel. Third, the one who hears the gospel receives the belief of the gospel, which is God's belief, or God's faith.

In other words, when a preacher comes and preaches, someone hears. What he hears gives him the right to believe it. If it has the power that will set him free—if it is the Word of God—then when he believes it and acts on it, he will be saved.

So, whoever will, may come. And whoever believes in this truth will not be put to shame, because when he believes in Christ and confesses Him as Lord, he will most assuredly be saved. (vv. 9,11,13.)

> *We can only receive God results with God's faith.*

Now, again, Paul said all this to emphasize one specific point: the way to receive salvation. A person cannot work up his own natural believing to get himself to heaven any more than the Jews Paul addressed could be saved by strictly adhering to Mosaic Law.

We cannot receive God results with natural, human faith or natural works. We can only receive God results with God's faith.

RECEIVE THE WORD, RECEIVE HIS FAITH

In Romans 10:15-16, Paul continued his message about receiving the God result of salvation:

It is written, How beautiful are the feet of them that preach the gospel of peace, and bring glad tidings of good things! But they have not all obeyed the gospel. For Esaias saith, Lord, who hath believed our report?

"They have not all obeyed the gospel," Paul said. Another translation says, "They have not all *received* the gospel." In other words, not everyone who hears the gospel receives it.

The deciding factor in whether or not one can receive the God-kind of faith is whether he rejects or accepts the gospel that he hears. As long as he is open and receptive to the Word, God's faith in that Word goes right to his spirit. Jesus explains this in the parable of the sower in Matthew 13:3-9. The explanation Jesus gave for the parable begins in verses 18 and 19:

> Hear ye therefore the parable of the sower. When any one heareth the word of the kingdom, and understandeth it not, then cometh the wicked one, and catcheth away that which was sown in his heart. This is he which received seed by the way side (Matthew 13:18,19).

Jesus said that this person heard the Word, yet lacked *understanding.* However, notice that the seed was sown in the *heart.* He actually received the seed. Even when our understanding is darkened, if the heart is receptive to the Word

> *Continuing to hear the word will water the seed and fortify your effectiveness as a doer of the Word.*

preached, the Word of faith, like a seed, goes directly to our heart. The heart is not only where faith is *received*, but also where it is *released*.

Why would the devil immediately respond by stealing the seed? It is a threat to him. This is why the Apostle Paul put so much emphasis on the Christian's understanding being enlightened. A saturation of the Word will produce a greater confidence and boldness in faith.

Let me illustrate it this way. I have two daughters, ages six and four. The oldest understands things that the four-year old has not learned. However, if both of the girls respond to the same request, whether or not they understand it, their response in obedience will receive my blessing. Further, if *understanding* is always necessary before we can receive, then how would you or I receive the baptism in the Holy Spirit?

Jesus very obviously knew that the power to produce was in the seed. He continually stressed being a doer of the Word of God. When the seed is sown you have it.

Continuing to hear the Word will water the seed and fortify your effectiveness as a doer of the Word. (John 1:8).

FAITH COMES WHEN YOU HEAR

We have looked at the salvation message in Romans 10 up to the point where we find a commonly used text for the message of faith, Romans 10:17. In this verse, Paul wrote, "So then faith cometh by hearing, and hearing by the word of God."

Was Paul saying that faith comes by hearing, and hearing, and hearing, and hearing? How would we explain that when this statement is in the context of Paul's message of salvation?

When a minister preaches the gospel to someone who is ready to receive salvation, does he say to that person, "Wait a second—you haven't heard it enough"?

"But I want to receive."

"You haven't heard it enough."

"Well, when will I be ready?"

"After you hear it enough, something will go off in your heart, and you'll know you're ready."

No. I don't know of any minister who would say that.

Neither does the Word of God say that.

The Bible says, "So then faith cometh by hearing, and hearing by the word of God." *The Amplified Bible* says it this way: "So faith comes by hearing [what is told], and what is heard comes by the preaching [of the message that came from the lips] of Christ (the Messiah Himself)."

In other words, when we hear God's Word, we receive His faith. That is why Paul told the Jews, "You ought to know that if you're hearing the message, then you're receiving the faith of God for your salvation. Confess what you're receiving and believe on the Lord Jesus Christ, and you will be saved." (vv. 8,9.)

This is the good news to the sinner: *God loves you. He believes in you. He has saved you. He brought you into fellowship with Himself through Jesus Christ. He has set you apart. He has given you His faith, for "faith cometh by hearing, and hearing by the Word of God" (Rom. 10:17). He's waiting for you to confess Him as Lord so that you can walk in that, but through His eyes of faith it is already done.*

Chapter Five

Have God's Faith

❧

And Jesus answering saith unto them, Have faith in God (Mark 11:22).

The Bible contains thorough evidence of God's faith. For example, God's faith enabled Him to form the worlds, as shown in Genesis 1. Verse 3 contains His first recorded words of faith: "Let there be light."

Do you know what God's faith did at that moment? The invisible made something visible. When God spoke those words of faith in the midst of darkness, the Word created the light. (John 1:1-3.)

HAVE FAITH IN GOD

Indeed, Jesus also has faith. The Gospels show us that while Jesus was on the earth, He used His faith continually. In Mark 11, for instance, we find Jesus using His faith to speak to a fig tree.

> And seeing a fig tree afar off having leaves, he came, if haply he might find any thing thereon: and when he came to it, he found nothing but leaves; for the time of figs was not yet.
>
> And Jesus answered and said unto it, No man eat fruit of thee hereafter for ever (Mark 11:13,14).

Verse 20 tells us what the disciples saw the next day: "And in the morning, as they passed by, they saw the fig tree dried up from the roots."

Along with the other disciples, Peter had heard Jesus curse the fig tree the day before. So when he saw the results of Jesus' command, he said, "Master, behold, the fig tree which thou cursedst is withered away" (v. 21).

Imagine all the thoughts that must have been going through Peter's mind right then. Presumably for the first time in his life, he had seen evidence of a *tree* obeying a *man*. So when he said, "Master, behold, the fig tree which thou cursedst is withered away," I don't think he was just saying, "Wow! Look at that!" I believe he was saying, "Jesus, how did You do that?"

Jesus responded by saying, "Have faith in God." One time when I read this, the Lord said, *Notice what I didn't say.* So I accepted His challenge and looked at it—for a long time. Then all of a sudden this came to me: When I was in grammar school, I learned that you should always answer a question by rephrasing the question in the form of a statement. So if Peter asked, "Lord, how did You do that?" the grammatically proper response would have begun with "I did that by...."

Therefore, if Jesus had been answering this question in my grammar school, He might have said something like

"Well, I did that by My faith." But that is not at all how Jesus answered.

Notice, instead, what He did say: Have *faith in God.* In the margin of the *King James Bible* it says, "Have the faith of God." (Mark 11:22). Thus, rather than taking credit for this miracle, Jesus responded to Peter's inquiry by saying, "My Daddy's faith did that. You need to have the God-kind of faith to do that."

Well, if it were impossible for us to have the God-kind of faith, then Jesus wouldn't have said we could have it. "God is not a man, that he should lie" (Num. 23:19), so if He said we can have it, then we can have it.

GOD'S WORD DIRECTED JESUS' EVERY ACTION

You may be thinking, *Well, Jesus is God, so why did He talk about the faith of God? Why didn't He just say, "My faith"?*

Yes, it is true that Jesus is God. However, because He was walking as a man, He attributed everything He did to God. In this instance, He gave glory to the faith of God.

Throughout the Gospels, we find Jesus saying things like: "I can do nothing of Myself. Everything I see My Father do, I do." (John 5:19,30.)

Jesus received direct commands and instructions—direct Word—from His Father. We know from Romans 10:17 that faith comes by hearing, and hearing by the Word of God. Thus, Jesus used His Father's belief, or faith, to do everything.

On earth Jesus was absolutely dependent upon His Father's Word, not upon Himself and His own ability, because He did have flesh—and with that flesh came a will. His earthly will began to speak in the Garden of Gethsemane, where Jesus said, "Oh, Lord, let this

> *We must completely depend upon God's Word, or God's faith, to follow in Jesus' footsteps.*

cup pass from Me. Nevertheless, not My will but Yours be done." (Matt. 26:39.)

Jesus came not to do His own will but the will of His Father, and He successfully achieved His goal by living by the Word, or faith, of His Father.

Jesus lived to receive the results He did, and we need to live to receive what we need. We must completely depend upon God's Word, or God's faith, to follow in Jesus' footsteps.

We don't have to go on a long journey to find faith. Having faith is not a matter of working on our own beliefs and trying to build ourselves up to a pinnacle of under-standing so that we can receive a God result; although understand-ing is very important to the action of faith.

We are responsible for the stewardship of our faith toward God.

No, faith has to come in a dif-ferent manner. As we consider the subject of faith coming to our hearts, we must remember that not all faith comes by hearing. Indeed, as it was presented in chapter 3, faith for salvation does come by hearing. The faith we as believers possess is the God-kind of faith; however, we are responsible for the stewardship of our faith toward God.

In I Corinthians 12:8-10 Paul addresses the church to clarify the regular or more common ways the Holy Spirit moves. Paul lists nine manifestations of the Spirit which include the word of wisdom, word of knowledge, special faith, gift of healings, working of miracles, prophecy, discerning of spirits, divers kinds of tongues, and interpretation of tongues. These manifestations all are given as the Holy Spirit wills. Faith, or *special* faith, which is God's ability for you to receive your miracle, comes as a gift or endowment operating through an individual believer. This explanation is proof that not all faith comes by hearing. What makes special faith unique is that God is the steward of this faith. The faith we as believers possess is the same God-kind of faith; however, we are responsible for the stewardship of our faith toward God.

GOD'S WORD IS HIS HEART

The only way we can obtain His faith is to receive it as a gift from Him. Romans 10:17 says, we receive God's faith through His Word: "Faith cometh by hearing, and hearing by the word of God."

Grace is God's ability to do for you what you can't do for yourself.

We know Romans 10:17 is addressed to the unbeliever—someone who needs to be born again. The only way we can obtain His faith is to receive it as a gift from Him.

Consider Eph. 2:8,9, "For by grace we are saved through faith; and that not of yourselves, it is the gift of God—not of works, lest any man should boast." Notice the word *gift*. Is this referring to grace, salvation, or faith? I think you will agree that it refers to each benefit or work of God equally.

In order to be saved you need to hear the Gospel preached; at this point faith comes. This faith is definitely

God's faith, so therefore a gift from God. With faith in action, as one *calls* on the name of the Lord, you access grace. Grace is God's ability to do for you what you can't do for yourself; obviously, this is a gift. Last but not least, grace produces salvation; something God purchased for you at the expense of His Son. Again, the same conclusion—a gift from God!

The faith of God comes to us as a gift from God. Whether you receive faith by hearing, before you are saved, as an endowment of *special faith* for service, or faith to live the Christian walk, when you are saved it is all a gift. The distribution may be different, however, the getting of faith is all from God!

In Romans 12:3 Paul wrote that God dealt to each one *the* measure of faith, meaning the measure He gave each person is the same measure.

> *When you act on the belief that comes from God, then it also includes His ability and faithfulness to bring it to pass.*

When I look at the word *dealt,* it reminds me of being dealt cards. Once those cards are dealt to me, they are mine to use during the game. Although those cards don't actually belong to me, the dealer gave me the right to use them when he dealt them to me. Even the other players acknowledge that: They might say to me, "How's *your* hand?"

The same concept applies to the way God deals us faith. God deals you the God-kind of faith through your hearing the Gospel and your salvation experience. That faith comes in a huge measure to live inside of you. It is God's faith in you, but you get to use it.

This might help you to understand why Jesus said on many occasions, "Thy faith hath made you well." The belief they embraced was God's will for their lives. You could say they embraced God's belief, or became a recipient of God's faith. They might not have been born again, yet when you act on the belief that comes from God, then it also includes His ability and faithfulness to bring it to pass. In other words, it is God's faith. After all, if we needed to be born again to use God's faith, then how would we become born again?

For as we have many members in one body, and all members have not the same office: so we, being many, are one body in Christ, and every one members one of another. Having then gifts differing according to the grace that is given to us,

> *It's not the proportion of the faith that you possess; it's the proportion you use.*

whether prophecy, let us prophesy according to the proportion of faith (Romans 12:4-6).

At first glance, you may look at this Scripture and think, *This seems to say that God gave faith to some in a lesser measure and to others in a greater measure.* But if you take a closer look, what this verse really says is that what God gives by measure are "gifts differing according to the *grace* that is given to us." But God gives everyone faith in the same measure.

The last statement in verse 6, "according to the proportion of faith," means according to the proportion of faith *that you use.* It's not the proportion of the faith that you possess; it's the proportion you use.

When God dealt to each one the *measure of faith,* we each received the same measure. Remember, it is not *a* measure of faith, but *the* measure of faith.

Jesus frequently said, *"Your* faith has made you whole." When a person has God's belief about something, that person has God's faith. When that person acts on, or uses, God's belief, then it becomes theirs in application.

If we are to remain in context for this passage of Scripture in Romans 12, then it should be clear that as Ephesians 4 says, God is distributing gifts to the body of Christ. Some people call these gifts the motivational gifts to the body of Christ. Not every member receives the same grace, or gifting. However, everyone does receive the same amount of faith.

Now, would God give us a measure of faith that was insufficient to fully function within our grace? No, this would be inconsistent with the way God gives anything. Remember, James 1:5 says that God is a *liberal* giver. Furthermore, 2 Corinthians 3:5 says that our sufficiency is not of ourselves but of God. In other words, with each different gift God has given us, He has amply supplied enough faith to completely operate in them as He intended.

Chapter Six

The Fruit of the Spirit

❧

B ut the fruit of the Spirit is love, joy, peace, longsuffering, gentleness, goodness, faith, meekness, temperance: against such there is no law (Galatians 5:22,23).

Thus far, I have presented several ideas from Scripture about the topic of faith. These are some of the biblical concepts presented: (1) God makes us believers; (2) faith comes by hearing His Word; (3) to the unsaved, faith is a gift at the new birth; (4) we are faith beings with the faith of God to live by; and (5) not all faith comes by hearing: special faith is a gift. Now, I want to focus on the idea faith is not only a gift from God; it actually becomes one of the fruits of the re-created human spirit.

As we found in chapter 3, God's kind of faith comes when we hear the Word, because the Word is God's heart and is full of faith. We receive saving faith when we hear the Gospel so that we can become born again. When we become born again, God annihilates our old nature and makes us brand new inside. He comes to live inside of us to make us His abode. The Holy Spirit takes up residence within us.

> *When we became one with God—so much so that all of our liabilities became His, and all of His assets become ours.*

When the Holy Spirit comes to dwell within us, He brings with Him character and attributes. Galatians 5:22,23 calls those things "the fruit of the Spirit."

But the fruit of the Spirit is love, joy, peace, long-suffering, gentleness, goodness, faith, meekness, temperance: against such there is no law.

These are the qualities of the divine-natured, God-possessed being. When we became born again, we became one with God—so much so that all of our liabilities became His, and all of His assets become ours. First Corinthians 6:17 confirms this, saying that we have become one spirit with Him.

The first asset Galatians 5:22 tells us about is God's love. That is a lot of love! He doesn't just possess love; 1 John 4:8 says, "God *is* love."

Therefore, if we are born again, we already have all the love we could ever need. We know that because Romans 5:5 says, "The love of God is shed abroad in our hearts by the Holy Spirit which is given unto us." That means, if we truly need more love, we need to become born again.

Romans 5:5 doesn't say, "The love of John or Jane has been shed abroad in our hearts." It says the love of God Himself has been shed abroad in our hearts. We already have the love of God. What we need to do is start acting on it and let it out.

The only reason why, as Christians, we ever respond in anger is that our minds are not renewed to the love of God. Our minds are not thinking what God thinks.

That's why we study 1 Corinthians 13:4-7, which says that God's love in us is not vainglorious, does not puff itself up, counts no wrong against another, is kind, is patient, is gentle, and thinks the best of everyone. We study this not so that we will receive God's love—because we already have it—but so that we always express God's love in us.

This is one of the things that Peter had a difficult time with. Just before Jesus ascended into heaven, He talked with His disciples at the shore of the sea of Tiberias. In John 21:15-17, we see Jesus speaking to Peter. He said, "Do you love Me, Peter?"

Peter said, "Lord, You know I love You."

Jesus said, "Feed My lambs. Peter, do you love Me?"

"Well, Lord, You know I love You."

"Well, then feed My lambs. Peter, do you love Me?"

"Lord, You know I love You."

When we read this in the English language, we look at it and say, "What is going on with Jesus? Why did He ask the same question three times?" But when we see it in the Greek, it's absolutely understandable.

Jesus said, "Peter, do you *agape* Me?"

Peter said, "You know I *phileo* You."

He said again, "Peter, do you *agape* Me?"

"Well, Lord, you know I *phileo* You."

Agape is the love of God.[1] The love of God is not something you can find on the earth. It did not come from the fall of man. The love of God comes out of heaven. We can see this kind of love manifested in John 3:16, for example: "For God so loved the world that He sent Jesus into the earth."

Phileo, on the other hand, is brotherly love.[2] It is the best kind of love the world can offer. People in the world just have to love one another the best they can.

We can love our brothers, our sisters, or our neighbors with *phileo* all we want to; but if that is all we have, we will not get to heaven. We can stand before God and say, "Well, I loved my brother. I loved my sister. I loved my neighbor;" but He will say, "Were you born again? Did you receive Jesus as your Lord? Were you filled with *agape,* the love of God?"

His love and His fruits—which He gives us the moment we become born again—are the only ones that set us apart as His children.

WHAT ABOUT THE OTHER FRUITS?

The Holy Spirit shed His love abroad in our hearts. So we know we have the love of God.

What, then, can we conclude about the other fruits listed in Galatians 5:22-23? What about joy? Nehemiah

8:10 says, "The joy of the Lord is your strength." So we know we have God's joy for every situation.

What about peace? Are we expected to just work up peace the best we can to try to make ourselves feel comfortable about our surroundings and situations? Or is there a greater peace than that?

Paul wrote in Philippians 4:7, "The peace *of* God, which passeth all understanding, shall keep your hearts and minds through Christ Jesus." It does not say, "Your own peace will guard your hearts and minds," but it says "the peace *of* God" will.

> *His peace came into our spirits in a more-than-enough measure.*

God gave us a divine nature, and then He said: "Peace I leave with you, my peace I give to you; not as the world gives give I unto you. Let not your heart be troubled, neither let it be afraid" (John 14:27).

No matter how impossible our situations may seem, God says, "I gave you My peace." It would be erroneous to say, "Jesus said to have peace, so I'm just going to try to have it." We don't have to try to have it. We have it! He placed it inside of our spirits. It came with our salvation.

And, just like the rest of His attributes, His peace came into our spirits in a more-than-enough measure. When we enter heaven, it will be easier to express God's peace because our minds won't be influenced by this earthly life. But when we enter heaven, God will not say, "Now I give you the fullness of My peace." He doesn't need to do that. He has *already* given us the fullness of every fruit of the spirit.

> *God placed all of His nature inside of us when we received His gift of salvation.*

And if the list of the fruits of the spirit begins with God's attributes, then it has to end the same way. Thus, when we get to "faith" in Galatians 5:23, we know it's not talking about human faith, or trying to work up some belief. One of the fruits He gave us is His faith. So just as confidently as we can say we have the love of God or the peace of God, we can also say we have the faith of God.

For too long, many Christians have thought, *I have to work on obtaining "some" faith.* What a sour deal that would be if we had all of these great attributes in us but had to find some faith to make them work. That is not the system God developed for us to operate in. That would be the same as "dangling a carrot before the mule" if God did that to His children. That does not sound like the love of God.

God doesn't make us work on our own attributes until they look like His. That would be the same as expecting us to work up our own salvation. And that is an inconceivable thing. On the contrary, God fills us with His faith. We are, however, responsible for developing that faith with His Word and to live in fellowship with Him.

Half the battle for most people is to know that we *already* have faith. God placed all of His nature inside of us when we received His gift of salvation. That nature automatically elevated us above everything the devil ever has done or ever will do. At the same time, God more than sufficiently supplied us with His own faith.

Some versions of Galatians 5:22,23 translate the word *faith* as *faithfulness.* So let me address this issue, just in case there is someone thinking that the word *faith* really means *faithfulness.* The Greek word *pistis* in *Strong's* is the same for *faith* or *faithfulness.* And if *faithfulness* were correct, then what is the faithfulness of God? It is God's ability to bring to pass what He's promised, so this would indicate that we have the ability of God in us to bring to pass what God has promised, just as God would do.

When we look at the fruits of the Spirit, we are looking at God's attributes, which came right out of heaven. Now, that doesn't mean that people in this world can't simulate these qualities. They can love, for example, but they are limited to *phileo,* brotherly love, and cannot express *agape,* the love of God.

> *We need to understand that God's attributes are ours, and therefore, we cannot fail.*

Our human attributes don't carry the same potency, or substance, as God's. The attributes of the human nature are from this world, so they can only do so much and they have temporal effectiveness. But the fruits of the Spirit are from the eternal world; therefore, they are omnipotent and have eternal effectiveness.

There is something in us as a born-again believer that is different from anything else in the world. God changed our nature, and now we are able to contain the very person of God Himself.

God's nature is inside of us, allowing us to do things that God Himself can do. Jesus said: "He that believeth on me, the works that I do shall he do also; and greater works than these shall he do; because I go unto my Father" (John 14:12).

He wanted us to know that the Holy Spirit was coming to change our nature, make us brand new, get inside of us, and place everything of God inside of us, including the Holy Spirit Himself. Thus, on this earth we are able to utilize everything Jesus has and do even greater things than He did.

If we believe this and let it be true in our lives, people will look at us and say, "These people look like Jesus!"

WE CANNOT FAIL

We need to understand that God's attributes are ours, and therefore, we cannot fail. Too many believers have been beaten down with faith-failure-consciousness. In other words, they have times when they believe God, and it seems they don't receive the answer they've expected. So when they're confronted with something that is a little bit bigger, the devil sits on their shoulders and says, *Your faith didn't work back then. Why do you think you're going to get it to work right now?*

Then these believers think they had better go back to square one and really start working at it and trying to build up their faith. They think, *I guess I don't have enough faith. So now I'm going to really work hard to get more faith. I haven't listened to enough tape series yet. I only read my Bible through once. Great men of faith usually read it through more than that. I've been a little lax today on my confession; I only said it about thirty times.*

What does that sound like? It sounds like works. It sounds like the "old" traditional thinking that calls us *unrighteous wretches* who must work and work to be good enough.

We know that's certainly not true, because, as Romans 10 explains, we've become righteous through faith. Furthermore, 2 Corinthians 5:21 says that we are the righteousness of God in Christ.

But some of us have applied traditional thinking to the subject of faith itself. We think, *Someday when I get faith I'll really be able to make a mountain move.* So we're working and working to get it to work. And in the midst of that struggle of works, it's not working. So our problem convinces us that we just don't have faith, that it's still not working. So we think, *Work harder. Try to get it. I'm not working hard enough.*

But Galatians 5:22,23 makes it clear that if we are reborn, we already have faith. And it is God's faith, which never fails. It is something we possess and something we are experts at, so we just work it.

Chapter Seven

No Faith, Little Faith, Great Faith

For I say, through the grace given unto me, to every man that is among you, not to think of himself more highly than he ought to think; but to think soberly, according as God hath dealt to every man the measure of faith (Romans 12:3).

God has given all of us the same measure of faith to use, but it seems that Jesus contrasted between one person's faith and another's. Let's look at some specific passages and see why this seeming contradiction in Scripture is really an invitation to discover God's design for our use of His faith.

I want to show you three places in Scripture in which the same story is told as seen through the eyes of three different writers: Matthew, Mark, and Luke. As you look at the story of Jesus calming the storm, I want you to see that each writer recorded Jesus' words differently.

MARK'S INTERPRETATION

Let's start with Mark 4:35-38:

And the same day, when the even was come, he saith unto them, Let us pass over unto the other side. And when they had sent away the multitude, they took him even as he was in the ship. And there were also with him other little ships. And there arose a great storm of wind, and the waves beat into the ship, so that it was now full. And he was in the hinder part of the ship, asleep on a pillow.

In this passage we see mighty wind and waves beating on the ship that Jesus and His disciples are in. But Jesus exercised such mastery over anything that was inconsistent with or contrary to the will of God so that He fell asleep on a pillow.

That's the way we should be when circumstances try to toss us around. When we know we possess the God-kind of faith, which always brings the answer, we will not be moved.

Verses 38-40 say:

And they awake him, and say unto him, Master, carest thou not that we perish? And he arose, and rebuked the wind, and said unto the sea, Peace, be still. And the wind ceased, and there was a great calm. And he said unto them, Why are ye so fearful? how is it that ye have no faith?

According to Mark, Jesus responded to the disciples' doubt by saying, "How is it that you have no faith?"

MATTHEW'S INTERPRETATION

Let's see how Matthew recorded Jesus' same statement. Matthew 8:26 says, "Why are ye fearful, O ye of little faith?"

Already we can see a contradiction between these two renderings of Jesus' statement: Mark wrote, "You don't have any faith at all." But Matthew wrote, "You only have a little bit of faith. *No* faith and a *little* faith are two entirely different things.

LUKE'S INTERPRETATION

Now let's look at a third rendering to see how Doctor Luke recorded these words. Luke 8:25 says, "Where is your faith?"

Let's put all three interpretations together now. Mark wrote, "You don't have any faith at all." Matthew wrote, "You only have a little bit of faith." And Luke wrote, "Where is your faith?"

Each of these three statements is different than the other, and yet each is from the same story. This means there is a deeper meaning than we can see on the surface.

I wanted to find out what that deeper meaning was, so I studied this topic in several dictionaries and commentaries. The commentaries agreed on this one reality: Jesus was not saying, "How is it that you have no faith?" He was saying, "How is it that *with your faith you use none?*"

Now, that would explain why Matthew said, "O ye of little faith." In other words, this meant "You're using faith with little effort" or "You're not putting much effort into using your faith."

That would explain why Mark said, "How is it that ye have no faith?" Jesus was asking, "Why are you using none of your faith?"

That would also explain why Luke said, "Where is your faith?" In other words, "If you have faith, where is it? Why aren't you using it? Where is the evidence of it?"

We know this is how Luke thought, because his record is steeped in this level of understanding. For instance, if you'll recall, when Jesus was preaching and the power of the Lord was present to heal all and the man was carried by his friends to the house and let down through the tiling, Luke said, "He [Jesus] saw their faith" (Luke 5:20).

Clearly Luke perceived faith as something that can and needs to be seen. This was also how James perceived faith. He said, "You say you have faith, but I'll *show* you what my faith does." (James 2:18.)

Later in the gospel of Luke, the author interpreted Jesus' words in this way: "When the Son of man cometh, shall he find faith on the earth?" (Luke 18:8). Well, of course He will find faith itself, but Luke was asking, "Will He find the action of faith? Will anyone be doing anything with His faith?"

"Why don't you use your faith?"

DOES FAITH ONLY COME IF YOU HEAR IT ENOUGH?

So, according to Matthew, Mark, and Luke respectively,

Jesus said to the disciples, "You're not putting much effort into using your faith;" "You only have a little bit of faith;" "You don't have any faith at all;" and "Where is your faith," or, in other words, "Why don't you use your faith?"

If faith only comes if you hear it enough, then we have a real dilemma, because no one heard the Word more than the disciples. They lived with the walking and talking Word. They walked with the Word in the flesh. They listened to the Word of God incarnate. John said, "We've handled the Word of life." (1 John 1:1.)

For the three and one-half years the disciples knew Jesus, it must have been almost as if they were in spiritual boot camp. They ate, slept, and drank the things of God. They were constantly surrounded by the principles of the kingdom of heaven.

It seems that if simply hearing the Word enough would give a person enough faith, then the disciples, of all people, should have automatically known what to do and done it when the storm arose. They shouldn't have been thinking, *Now, what am I supposed to do.*

Matthew 8:5-10 poses another objection to the idea that faith only comes when we hear the Word enough.

And when Jesus was entered into Capernaum, there came unto him a centurion, beseeching him, and saying, Lord, my servant lieth at home sick of the palsy, grievously tormented. And Jesus saith unto him, I will come and heal him.

The centurion answered and said, Lord, I am not worthy that thou shouldest come under my roof: but speak the word only, and my servant shall be healed. For I am a man under authority, having soldiers under me: and I say to this man, Go, and he goeth; and to another, Come, and he cometh; and to my servant, Do this, and he doeth it.

When Jesus heard it, he marvelled, and said to them that

> *The greatness of his faith was the way he used what he heard.*

followed, Verily I say unto you, I have not found so great faith, no, not in Israel.

Now we have another dilemma. If we have to hear and hear the Word before faith drops down in our hearts or increases to become "great faith," then this centurion broke the rules. He didn't go to the synagogue. He didn't spend time meditating on God. So how did he acquire this great faith?

To understand this, we need to separate the words *great* and *faith*. They are, in fact, two words.

The *faith* part is really easy to explain: He heard about Jesus, and the God-kind of faith came, just as it always does.

The *great* part, however, he acquired not in the synagogue, but in the military. The greatness of his faith, you see, was the way he used what he heard. This man used what he heard properly because, from his military training, he understood submission and authority. Therefore, when he heard about Jesus, he esteemed Him as a man under a supernatural authority because the works that He did were supernatural. He said:

I am not worthy that thou shouldest come under my roof: but speak the word only, and my servant shall be healed. For I am a man under authority, having soldiers under me: and I say to this man, Go, and he goeth; and to another, Come, and he cometh; and to my servant, Do this, and he doeth it.

Essentially, he said, "I believe You are under authority. As a man who is under authority, I know that when I speak, authority above me causes people to comply. Therefore, You don't need to come under my roof. If You will just speak the Word, my servant will be healed in submission to the authority above You."

The centurion wasn't looking at the symptoms when he heard about Jesus and the things Jesus did. He was fixed on the authority above Jesus: He was looking to God. He was looking to a supernatural substance, a supernatural personality. He was looking forward in faith, knowing that if Jesus would just speak a word under that authority, the symptoms in his servant would have to submit and disappear.

The way he used his faith was great, so Jesus marveled and said, "I have not seen such great faith even in Israel."

> *It is not in our own ability to make our faith big enough to meet the task.*

Isn't it sad that Jesus had to go over to the Roman military to find great faith, when the Jews were steeped in a tradition of believing God and witnessing the manifestation of His power? Even after all of their experiences with God, the Jews did not know how to use their faith in a great way, as did this military man.

WE CAN'T MAKE OUR FAITH BIG ENOUGH

This story disproves the theory that so many believers cling to. They think they have to hear and hear the Word to build up a huge amount of faith so they can say, "Now I have sufficient faith to master this particular task."

It is true that we should want to hear and hear the Word to strengthen our positions of faith. The more we consider the victory in the Word, the more our minds are enlightened. But we must realize that it is not in our own ability to make our faith big enough to meet the task. God has given us more than enough ability: He has given us His own ability, His own faith, and His own power to meet the task. The greatness we need to aspire to is not in the level of our faith. We are all at the same more-than-enough level—but it is reflected in the way we use it.

That's why Jesus said to the disciples, "How is it that *with your faith you use none?*" Their faith didn't have a problem: It was the God-kind of faith. The problem was in the way they used it. "Oh, Master, look at the winds and the waves," they said, looking hopelessly at the negative natural circumstances.

Apparently the disciples had grown up with a failure mentality. Jesus had said, "Let us cross to the other side." (Mark 4:35.) His word alone was more than sufficient to take them there. We know that because when Peter said, "Lord, if it be You, bid me come," Jesus' word, "Come," enabled Peter to walk on the water. (Matt. 14:28,29.)

However, despite their eyewitness proof of the ability of Jesus' word, the disciples' ability to use their faith weakened as soon as opposition arose. They started crying, "Oh, Jesus, what are we going to do? Don't You care? I can't believe You're on the pillow sleeping, and we are here fighting these waves!" (That was the problem: They were fighting something that had already been conquered.) That's why Jesus asked in amazement, "Why don't you use your faith?"

There are only two stories in Scripture where we find Jesus talking about "great faith." The first one was the story of a Roman military officer, who was a Gentile. The second one is the story of a Canaanite woman, another Gentile. This story is found in Matthew 15:21-28:

> Then Jesus went thence, and departed into the coasts of Tyre and Sidon. And, behold, a woman of Canaan came out of the same coasts, and cried unto him, saying, Have mercy on me, O Lord, thou Son of David; my daughter is grievously vexed with a devil. But he answered her not a word.

And his disciples came and besought him, saying, Send her away; for she crieth after us. But he answered and said, I am not sent but unto the lost sheep of the house of Israel.

Then came she and worshipped him, saying, Lord, help me. But he answered and said, It is not meet to take the children's bread, and to cast it to dogs. And she said, Truth, Lord: yet the dogs eat of the crumbs which fall from their masters' table. Then Jesus answered and said unto her, O woman, great is thy faith: be it unto thee even as thou wilt. And her daughter was made whole from that very hour.

We know this woman received the God-kind of faith because she heard about Jesus. But what caused Jesus to say, "great"? Where did she get "great" faith?

She didn't grow up in church. She grew up in a heathen society—a tough place where, according to history, thieves would rob people blind in a heartbeat. A person growing up in such an environment would quickly learn, *If I'm going to have anything, I have to go after it.* Her skin was tough, so to speak. No matter what anyone said, she went after what she needed and, once she got it, she held on to it.

This was the woman's character. She came using a borrowed phrase, "Have mercy on me, Lord, Son of David." I can imagine her going to someone moments before and asking, "Hey, wait a second. What is that phrase they use to get His attention?"

When she used this borrowed phrase, Jesus didn't even answer her because it was not the right thing for her to say. So, in essence, He helped her to receive her faith by being very direct with her. "You're not of the lost sheep of the house of Israel."

> *The greatness of her belief was in her determination not to give up.*

Then she humbled herself and said from her heart, "Oh, Lord." And she fell down and worshiped Him.

But Jesus said, "I still can't give you the children's bread."

She said, "Well, listen, I don't care what you call me. If you call me a dog, even the crumbs that fall from the Master's table are for the dogs to eat. You're the Master, and You have something I desire. My daughter is going to be well."

Jesus said, "O woman, great is thy faith: be it unto thee even as thou wilt." In other words, "May it be as you have determined," or "according to the power of your will.

So we can see that the greatness of her belief was in her determination not to give up.

JESUS COMMENDED DETERMINATION

We find such determination commended elsewhere in the Scriptures. For example, in Luke 11:5-8 Jesus told a parable of a man's prayer of importunity, in which he essentially said to the keeper of the house, "Hey, I need something right now."

He replied, "Well, we've all gone to bed, and we can't come help you."

But he kept on knocking and knocking and knocking. And though the man didn't want to come to the door, for the sake of some peace and quiet, he came and gave him what he needed.

That is called determination. He did not let up until he got what he needed.

So many people just go a little way with God and then, if nothing has changed, they give up. That's not determination! That is not the way to use faith. If we want to operate faith in a *great* way, determination must be a quality in our lives.

If we will use the faith of God with the determination of all heaven, the power of the Word will back up that faith and deliver a God-result every time.

PAUL'S DETERMINATION

That's how the apostle Paul lived out his faith. In Acts 14:19-21, Luke recorded a story that reveals Paul's determination in the faith:

And there came thither certain Jews from Antioch and Iconium, who persuaded the people, and, having stoned Paul, drew him out of the city, supposing he had been dead. Howbeit, as the disciples stood round about him, he rose up, and came into the city: and the next day he departed with Barnabas to Derbe. And when they had preached the gospel to that city, and had taught many, they returned again to Lystra, and to Iconium, and Antioch.

Now, I want you to see the picture here. Paul was stoned, and then he went back into the same city. Why would he do that? Why would he want to bless a city where people did not even care whether he lived or died?

> *If we are "in the faith," we have come out of this world and have been translated into another world.*

The reason that he loved not his life to death was that there was a passion in his soul. What was that passion? Was it a desire to get people faith because he was worried that they hadn't received enough? No. Verse 22 tells us what his passion was: "Confirming the souls of the disciples, and exhorting them to continue in the faith." He wanted to strengthen them and encourage them to stay true to the faith they already had and were already in.

In the early church, believers were said to be "in the faith." You'll find that phrase "in the faith" over and over again in the epistles.

If we are "in the faith," not only does that mean we are in this particular belief; it also means that belief is in us. "The faith" is like a club that we join. The faith club, if you will, is comprised of every child of God. If we are "in the faith," we have come out of this world and have been translated into another world. We are now partaking and living out of that world.

If we are in the faith, then faith is in us. It's not a matter of finding out whether we have enough faith. It's a matter of doing something with our more-than-enough God-kind of faith.

Why would Paul go back to the same place where he was beaten up? He did so because he absolutely would not pass up an opportunity to once again encourage the believers, saying, "Stay with your faith. Persevere with it. March on with it. Use it. It will win. It will cause you to be victorious every time. Don't draw back; move on, because you're in the faith."

Paul showed us that we are champion believers. So, what should the character of a champion believer look like? Second Peter 1:5-7 shows us the attributes we need to develop to use the faith we have:

> And beside this, giving all diligence, add to your faith virtue; and to virtue knowledge; and to knowledge temperance; and to temperance patience; and to patience godliness; and to godliness brotherly kindness; and to brotherly kindness charity.

Notice, it doesn't say, "Add to your faith more faith, because you don't have enough of it." No, it shows us the things we need to add to our faith so we can use it appropriately: virtue, knowledge, self-control, perseverance, godliness, brotherly kindness, and love.

Then verses 8-9 say:

For if these things be in you, and abound, they make you that ye shall neither be barren nor unfruitful in the knowledge of our Lord Jesus Christ. But he that lacketh these things is blind, and cannot see afar off, and hath forgotten that he was purged from his old sins.

If these things abound in us, then we will be fruitful in the knowledge of Jesus. And if our knowledge of Jesus is fruitful, then we understand that we have what the Word of God says we have.

> *The way people think about themselves will determine the way they use their faith.*

However, if these things don't abound in us, then we won't see what God has provided. We will even forget that our old sins were wiped away.

That is why we must be fortified in virtue, knowledge, self-control, perseverance, godliness, brotherly kindness, and love. These attributes define the champion believer.

Know Who You Are so You Can Fight

This is the way Paul talked to people. Paul's main theme concerning faith throughout his letters to the churches, was "fight the good fight of faith." (1 Tim. 6:12.) Do we fight the good fight of faith by just constantly speaking about it until we are sure we have enough and we qualify to use it? No, Paul said, "Fight the good fight of faith, *lay hold on eternal life.*"

Paul didn't constantly speak about faith. Instead, he talked continually about who we are and what we have in Christ. He talked about who God is and who we are in God.

This builds the character of the hearer to step up and be a God person and use His faith. The way people think about themselves will determine the way they use their faith.

Paul understood that when we show someone how important he is in Christ and how much ability he has in Christ, through one Scripture after another, we begin to build God's case that a believer must win. If a believer with the faith of a champion will just step out and begin to act on what he has, it will work every time.

We need a new perspective of the gifts God has given us—especially of His faith. Here is a simple illustration about the importance of perspective.

If all day long I kept telling my child, "Don't touch the cookie jar," then you can be sure; this would become the most difficult thing for her not to do. Why? Because I put in her "a cookie-jar" mentality. She was being constantly reminded—made to think—about the cookie jar. Now, the real issue is not the cookie jar. The issue is obedience. If I had taken the time to help her understand my command from the perspective of her obedience, that it is pleasing to God and to her daddy, then the cookie jar would never be a problem.

A faith-failure mentality is developed in many believers because they spend so much time trying to make sure they have *some* faith and that their faith is good enough to qualify them for God's gifts. Thus, they are convinced the problem in their lives is *faith*.

We are believers! We are faith people! We are not of those who draw back. We are a holy people, a royal priesthood! We are chosen vessels! We choose to use His faith in a great way to receive what God says we have, and *His* faith in us brings *His* results every time!

Chapter Eight

Qualified

❧

G iving thanks to the Father who has qualified us to be partakers of the inheritance of the saints in the light (Colossians 1:12 NKJV).

Through the work of the Cross and our response to God's Word—His faith—we have received the gift of reconciliation with God. Not only did His gift make us the righteousness of God in Christ and fill us with all of God's nature, but it also qualified us for every gift God has ever promised in His Word.

Our frame of mind affects the outcome of everything we do.

However, it seems few believers remember the work God has done in and for them. Few believers approach life as the champions they are in Christ.

Our frame of mind affects the outcome of everything we do. That is why it has been my goal through this book to help you break free from the mental bondage that has made you feel unqualified because of past "faith failures." If you are bound by that mentality, then you will never use God's faith as He intended you to.

The devil would like to bombard you with all kinds of reasons why you can't use your faith. But God wants to bombard your mind with every reason why it's impossible that you couldn't use His faith: God is for you, and no one can be against you (Rom. 8:31); you can do all things through Christ who strengthens you. (Phil. 4:19.)

I want you to imagine that God's faith is the fastest, best handling vehicle on earth, and it is the vehicle you are in now as a believer. Imagine also that it doesn't matter if you've never operated this vehicle before or if you've never had a victory before; you can drive God's vehicle and you will take the checkered flag every single time you get in because it is made just for you. It's going to outdo anything this world has.

We have to conform our thinking to the truth of the Word. We are already in the kingdom of God. We are already heirs to *all* the things of heaven. God has already given us *all* things that pertain to life and godliness. (2 Peter 1:3.) It's time to use them.

> *There is no compromise in the voice of a believer who absolutely believes what God said.*

As believers, we have the highest faith anyone can have—the God-kind—but we cannot use things when we don't *think* we can.

Some believers don't understand who they are. It's apparent in their words. You can see it in their demeanor. They do not have the demeanor of people who will end their race with the checkered flag in hand!

On the other hand, there is no compromise in the voice of a believer who absolutely believes what God said. He will not turn back on it. A person of such character will say, "If that is what the Word says, then that is what I have—right now."

ALREADY QUALIFIED

The Word says, "The Father...has qualified us to be partakers of the inheritance of the saints in the light" (Col. 1:12 NKJV). God has already qualified us for every gift He's ever promised in His Word to His people. There is nothing in God that we need to qualify for. Once we become born again, we already qualify.

A believer doesn't have to read enough books and hear enough sermons to qualify to be filled with the Holy Spirit, healed, financially prosper, and so forth. He is qualified right now. Why wait?

I'm not suggesting that because we have the faith of God we should cease to read the Word or pray. Quite the contrary, our relationship to God through His Word and prayer is our spiritual backbone. And it is only through that relationship that our faith can work to produce the results God desires for us.

Traditional thinking has taught people to believe that although God has performed the biggest miracle of all—that of salvation—they must work to qualify themselves to receive anything else from God. We received every promise of God when we became born again. Christ qualified us to partake of the inheritance of the saints in the light.

If Jesus qualified us, then we do not receive our inheritance by our own qualifications. We receive them by His qualification. That makes us an absolute success in everything we do. Jesus never had trouble receiving from His Father, and neither do we.

You are living by Christ's qualification. This is what Paul said in Galatians 2:20:

> I am crucified with Christ: nevertheless I live; yet not I, but Christ liveth in me: and the life which I now live in the flesh I live by the faith of the Son of God, who loved me, and gave himself for me.

"Christ lives in me," Paul said. That is the qualification for being a partaker.

Then he said, "I live by the faith of the Son of God." In other words, Paul was saying, "I live by God's faith, or the God-kind of faith."

Paul was not proclaiming anything that he was doing. He said, "I am no longer living." It was not his life that he was living. The life that was in him was Christ's. So the way that he received what he needed in life was by Christ's faith, God's faith.

God qualified him for everything. He was living Christ's life. He was living by the faith *of* God.

Now, if Paul had been living his own life, then he would have been trying to have faith in God. But because he was living Christ's life, he naturally lived by Christ's faith.

Paul was not living by any human faith either. In Romans 3:3 he asked, "For what if some did not believe? Shall their unbelief make the faith of God without effect? God forbid."

> *The battle is not about getting some faith; it's about conquering doubt so you can use God's faith effectively.*

We don't live by anyone's faith but God's. What anyone else does with God's faith is irrelevant in our lives. What *we* do with it is what matters.

You may have some problems with your mind doubting, but you cannot have a faith failure. James 1:5-7 says:

If any of you lack wisdom, let him ask of God, that giveth to all men liberally, and upbraideth not; and it shall be given him. But let him ask in faith, nothing wavering.

For he that wavereth is like a wave of the sea driven with the wind and tossed. For let not that man think that he shall receive any thing of the Lord.

The man who wavers is the man who allows doubt to step in. In other words, he allows his mind to step in and then his mind overrides his faith.

The mind is where the battleground is. The battle is not about getting some faith; it's about conquering doubt so you can use God's faith effectively. Your mind is the part of you that has accepted worldly ways and has elevated itself. It has been wearing the crown in your life, and it doesn't like to give up its kingship.

For example, your mind doesn't like to be told that though your body *feels sick,* you are really *healed* because Jesus took your sickness. (1 Peter 2:24.) It wants to tell your body, *You ought to just go ahead and lie down because you're just not feeling well.*

DON'T SUBMIT TO THE SYMPTOM

When my youngest daughter was two and a half years old, she had a cough for a couple of days. We ministered the life of God to her. One morning she came into the room where I was, and she just sat there and coughed. I looked over at her, and she looked up at me and just smiled and said, "Daddy, I'm healed by the name of Jesus."

She did not submit to that symptom in her body, and neither did I. I said, "Honey, that is exactly right. You are healed in the name of Jesus. Come to me." I put my hands on her and said, "In the name of Jesus, glory to God, this child is healed."

As believers we do not submit to *anything* but God and His Word. Jesus had to completely submit to His Father in order to utilize the power of God. Therefore, we also need to completely submit to the Father.

When you have pain, you ought to check up on Jesus. Say, "Doctor Jesus, what is that pain really saying right now?" You ought to have a close enough relationship with Him that you can hear Him say, *Well, child, what that means is there is an infection trying to attack your body right here. I took your infections, so don't worry about it. Just begin to praise and worship Me and you will see those symptoms disappear immediately.*

We need to live like Paul, who finished his course and the ministry, loving not his life even unto death. He was willing to die for the Gospel, including the reality that "Himself took my infirmities and bare my sicknesses" (Matt. 8:17).

I didn't say you should not go to a doctor. And I'm *not* telling you to stop taking your prescribed medication. God can heal you even while you're on that medication. He wants you healed because you are His child.

We just need to take out the clutter in our minds of how we ought to live and move and have our being, so that God can actually do something.

ARE YOU READY FOR A GOOD RUN?

I remember one day while I was ministering about God's life in us, a lady came up for prayer. She was filled with so much asthma that just to listen to her breathe would cause a person to become very nauseated. She was barely getting a breath. You wondered how her lungs could even get enough oxygen to get into the blood and cause the blood to have any life. So I said to her, really nonchalantly, "Well, glory to God! Are you ready for a good run?"

She looked at me and said, "I'm not running."

I looked at her and said, "Yes, you are. Are you ready for a run?"

She said, "I'm not running."

I looked at her and said, "Well, I'll give you two choices. One choice is, you run on your own. The second choice is, I will run you around this room."

> *You can't fail using God's faith.*

She looked at me, and tears welled up in her eyes. In a religious tone, she said, "Son, I just don't know that I have enough faith for that."

It seemed valid, but it wasn't the truth according to the Word. So I said, "Well, really, what you've got is the faith of God. Your faith doesn't qualify. It's His faith that qualifies. If you'll just use His faith as He used it, you'll get results just like He got. I don't care how many failures you think you've had in the past; you've never had a faith failure, because you can't fail using God's faith. You've had some head problems, but you don't have a heart problem."

She looked back at me with eyes as big as saucers and said, "Well, when are we running?"

I said, "Right now."

She took off running. She ran around the building and came back breathing clearly. She wasn't even out of breath. She was just shouting and praising God that her lungs could breathe. She was instantly healed.

Faith Is an Ongoing Action

The disciples learned the way of faith by observing the Master operate in it daily, moment by moment. They didn't learn it as a set of theories or rules and methods to push a button and pull a lever to get it to work. No, they learned that faith is an ongoing action. It is our life. It is our breath. It is something we'll live for and something we'll die for.

Luke called the book of Acts "the actions of the Holy Spirit through the New Testament church, or the acts of the apostles." The only thing these early apostles and believers thought about was action: *We believe this, so we're going to act it out. We've got something, so we are going to do something with it.*

Today so many Christians believe they are unqualified to receive anything from God and they have to go study a little bit more. So while they have their heads in some corner, seeing if they

> *When you know it's God's faith working in you, you won't let up.*

can get themselves to feel ready, they are letting their miracles pass them right by.

All they need to see is that they've been made in His image and in His likeness. They've been fashioned after Jesus, and they do what they're made to do: believe.

One woman, whose story is found in Mark 5, heard about Jesus and received God's faith. She took off running with it and began to say with her mouth, "If I just touch the hem of His garment, I will be well." When no one else could help her, the faith of God within her brought into reality supernatural power that changed her physical surroundings. She did it with the God-kind of faith.

When you know it's God's faith working in you, you won't let up. You can't be denied. You take on a different attitude. Attitude is everything. For example, when you get into a contest with someone else, your attitude toward the contest can destroy the other person's ability to perform.

Let's say, for instance, your favorite football team makes a couple successful plays right in a row. They could have been down by twenty points, but when the momentum swings over to their side, all of a sudden their attitudes change. They begin to put forth more effort, and their abilities increase, because they believe in themselves.

Likewise, when one person on a team starts to make some good plays and the next person starts to do the same, something happens in the atmosphere and everyone's attitude is raised to a higher level. Watch the team's ability increase.

By our attitudes, we create the environment around ourselves.

This works in a spiritual sense as well. When one believer starts to see results from God's faith within him, and another starts to see the same, something happens in the atmosphere and everyone's attitude and expectancy are raised to a higher level. Then the church's victory over the kingdom of darkness is made more and more evident in the earth.

Your attitude is your demeanor. It's what you express, without even speaking. It is so very important to have a good attitude. Even when you don't feel like it, give off a "good fragrance" to someone around you, for we are to God the fragrance of Christ among those who are being saved and among those who are perishing. (2 Cor. 2:15.)

By our attitudes, we create the environment around ourselves. We don't want our own ability mixed up in this thing; we want heaven's ability. We need to mix our faith, with an attitude of victory, a consciousness of triumph. When we do, *nothing* will stop us, for we are already qualified to receive every blessing included in the inheritance of the saints in the light.

Chapter Nine

Lay Hold on Eternal Life

❧

Fight the good fight of faith, lay hold on eternal life, whereunto thou art also called, and hast professed a good profession before many witnesses (1 Timothy 6:12).

"Fight the good fight of faith," wrote the apostle Paul.

Well, Paul, how are we going to fight the good fight of faith?

"Lay hold on eternal life," he responds.

Let me present an illustration to explain what Paul meant by this statement, "Lay hold on eternal life."

Imagine you find yourself hanging off a cliff over a deep gorge. To your dismay, the stone you caught hold of starts to break loose, the ground is breaking apart and pieces are falling around you. At any second you could die!

Now imagine that help comes and a rope is let down within your reach. A voice says, "Hold on to the rope!" At that moment your life depends on that rope. Will you cling to the rope or just hold on by a couple fingers, thinking, *I've got other things to think about?*

I don't think that is how you would react. You would grab that rope with both hands and squeeze so tightly that your knuckles would turn white. You'd hold on to that rope with every part of your being.

That is how Paul told us to hold on to the life of God. "Lay hold on eternal life," he said.

Do you want to fight the good fight of faith? Do you want to get in there and be victorious in the faith fight? If so, then how will you do it? You will hold on tightly to eternal life—God's divine nature and ability that Jesus said He has given you in great abundance:

> The thief cometh not, but for to steal, and to kill, and to destroy: I am come that they might have life, and that they might have it more abundantly (John 10:10).

Jesus said the thief, or the devil, wants to steal, kill, and destroy. What are the devil's methods? What is his armament? What is his power? What is his ability to steal, kill, and destroy?

According to Scripture, Jesus took the devil's power. He destroyed his works; He took the keys of his authority over us. In Revelation 1:18, Jesus said, "I am he that liveth, and was dead; and, behold, I am alive for evermore, Amen; and have the keys of hell and of death."

The devil doesn't have the keys of hell and death any longer. You have to understand this: Jesus defeated the devil 2000 years ago.

DECEPTION: THE DEVIL'S WEAPON

The devil comes to kill, steal, and destroy through deception. That's the way he started in the Garden of Eden. He didn't try to wrestle Adam or put him in a head-lock. Adam was a son of God, clothed in the very anointing of the Holy Spirit. If the devil had even come close to that anointing, it would have overpowered him.

> *Pride put Satan in a position to fall.*

Satan understood that anointing because he had experienced God's anointing on him when he was Lucifer in heaven. He was the greatest angelic being in God's kingdom. He walked around in the anointing, that holy clothing or covering that caused him to be the highest of all musicians and the most beautiful of all the angels.

Son of man, take up a lamentation upon the king of Tyrus, and say unto him, Thus saith the Lord GOD; Thou sealest up the sum, full of wisdom, and perfect in beauty. Thou hast been in Eden the garden of God; every precious stone was thy covering, the sardius, topaz, and the diamond, the beryl, the onyx, and the jasper, the sapphire, the emerald, and the carbuncle, and gold: the workmanship of thy tabrets and of thy pipes was prepared in thee in the day that thou wast created. Thou art the anointed cherub that covereth; and I have set thee so: thou wast upon the holy mountain of God; thou hast walked up and down in the midst of the stones of fire. Thou wast perfect in thy ways from the day that thou wast created, till iniquity was found in thee (Ezek. 28:12-15).

His downfall began when he started to think that somehow he had promoted himself to that position, when in fact it was the anointing that had caused him to be who he was. Pride put him in a position to fall.

The moment he became prideful, he lost that anointing and fell like lightning to the earth. (Luke 10:18.) Suddenly the devil understood what the anointing did and didn't do. In his fallen state he recognized that he was nothing without the anointing of God.

The devil knew that when God made Adam, He clothed him in the very glory of God. The first Adam looked just like the second Adam, who is Jesus.

What did Jesus' anointing look like? On the Mount of Transfiguration, He had such power that it came right out of his skin and transfigured Him into a glowing light. (Mark 9:2,3.)

"God is light, and in him is no darkness at all" (1 John 1:5). So, what do you think Adam looked like to the devil? Just like Jesus, Adam looked like light walking on the face of the earth.

However, the devil was unable to comprehend or to overcome and seize control of the light. John 1:4-5 says, "In him was life; and the life was the light of men. And the light shineth in darkness; and the darkness comprehended it not."

So at first the devil stayed a good distance away from Adam. But then, in order to inch his way into the very life of Adam and Eve, he had to deceive their minds.

If Adam had not submitted to Satan's deception, his body would never have died. God didn't make Adam's body mortal. He gave him a body that would live forever. Originally, Adam was a perfect human being who would live forever under God's direction—honoring, loving, and serving Him.

Adam served as God's under-shepherd, about whom one might use terminology that would scare most religious people. Let me explain. Over in 2 Corinthians 4:4, the devil is called the god of this world: "In whom the god of this world hath blinded the minds of them which believe not...." The only reason he is called "the god of this world" is that he has the rights and privileges of the lease on this world—the rights and privileges that God originally gave Adam.

Genesis 1:26-30 records God's delegation of authority over everything on the earth to Adam:

> And God said, Let us make man in our image, after our likeness: and let them have dominion over the fish of the sea, and over the fowl of the air, and over the cattle, and over all the earth, and over every creeping thing that creepeth upon the earth. So God created man in his own image, in the image of God created he him; male and female created he them.
>
> And God blessed them, and God said unto them, Be fruitful, and multiply, and replenish the earth, and subdue it: and have dominion over the fish of the sea, and over the fowl of the air, and over every living thing that moveth upon the earth.
>
> And God said, Behold, I have given you every herb bearing seed, which is upon the face of all the earth, and every tree, in the which is the fruit of a tree yielding seed; to you it shall be for meat. And to every beast of the earth, and to every fowl of the

air, and to every thing that creepeth upon the earth, wherein there is life, I have given every green herb for meat: and it was so.

Adam was the son of God. He was God's small g-o-d of this world. Though Adam was certainly not God, God made Adam just like Himself, with His ability to serve Him and act on His behalf in the earth. For instance, God gave Adam the authority to name all of the animals and birds He had made:

> And out of the ground the Lord God formed every beast of the field, and every fowl of the air; and brought them unto Adam to see what he would call them: and whatsoever Adam called every living creature, that was the name thereof. And Adam gave names to all cattle, and to the fowl of the air, and to every beast of the field (Genesis 2:19,20).

How did Adam have the capacity to do that? God gave him the capacity. It would have been foolish for God to delegate authority over everything He made to someone who was incapable of exercising that authority. Adam would not have done a very good job of naming those creatures without God's ability within him.

God fashioned Adam with that ability. He made Adam a spirit being who possessed an intellect, perfect in form and function, and inhabited a body that would never have a wrinkle or grow old.

SIN MADE HIM MORTAL

Then Satan began to work on Adam's helpmate, Eve, to weaken her to the point that she began to doubt what God had said and what God would do. There are two things a person can do to please God: (1) believe that He is, and (2) believe that when we seek Him, He'll diligently reward us. (Heb. 11:6.) Those are the very same things that the devil came against Eve with (and, consequently, Adam) in the Garden.

The only cure for mortality is immortality.

When Adam and Eve submitted themselves to sin, they became

mortal. They died spiritually and were separated from God. (Gen. 3:3,19.)

Later, when Jesus came as the second Adam, the same thing happened to Him that happened to Adam. He became mortal. That is why, when Jesus hung on the cross, the Father turned His back on His Son, and Jesus cried out, "My God, my God, why have You forsaken Me?" (Matt. 27:46). He was alone, because He chose to take our death to give us God's life.

The only cure for mortality is immortality. When Jesus arose from the grave, He arose completely immortal. In that glorified, immortal state, He was able to go through matter, to walk through doors. (John 20:19.)

If Jesus had not known He was able to go through matter, He would have reached for every doorknob, just as you and I do. But because He knew who He was, He was able to show His disciples that they had nothing to fear: No barrier could keep Him from meeting with those who loved Him.

In John 10:10, Jesus said that the counteraction to the devil's stealing, killing, and destroying through deception is God's life. He said, "I've come to give you this life in an abundant measure." We must see this! Jesus did not come to give life to us in a *small* measure so we would go through life just hoping and praying that someday He would come and get us out of this mess. On the contrary, He has come to give us life in an *abundant* measure that will go beyond what we could ever imagine.

This word *life* in the original Greek is zoe.[1] This is the very life of God. We have the very nature, life, and ability of God in us.

See then, if we know who we are and we hold on tightly to that abundance of the life of God within, we will fight to win. We will not be moved; we will not back up.

We'll end up taking a faith walk and fighting a great faith fight, but it won't be because we're thinking, *What am I supposed to say now? How am I supposed to say it? What faith button am I supposed to push? What lever am I supposed to pull?*

When a thief tries to steal a woman's purse, does she say, "Oh, go ahead and take it?"

Now, the woman does not walk down the street thinking about, *What will I do if a thief tries to take my purse?* She just goes about her business, and when the thief comes to steal from her what she knows is hers, she fights to hold on to it. Her success or victory has everything to do with how strong she is. But, our victory has everything to do with how strong God is!

That purse is like the zoe² life that I am talking about. It is ours. It belongs to us. It is the sustenance of our being. This life of God is the very reason we are able to operate in faith. The life of God is the reason Paul could go back to churches that he established and say with conviction from personal experience, "Stand fast in the faith," or in other words, "Be immovable in the faith." (1 Cor. 16:13.)

CHRIST IN YOU: THE GREAT MYSTERY

Paul stood immovably in the faith, and yet the wonder of Christ's life in believers still awed him. He wrote:

For we are members of his body, of his flesh, and of his bones. This is a great mystery: but I speak concerning Christ and the church (Ephesians 5:30,32).

The revelation of the great mystery of Christ and the Church is so extremely powerful and so profound that Paul returned to the thought frequently. In Colossians 1:26-27, he wrote: "Even the mystery which hath been hid from ages and from generations, but now is made manifest to his saints: to whom God would make known what is the riches of the glory of this mystery among the Gentiles; which is Christ in you, the hope of glory."

WHAT CAN GOD'S LIFE DO?

Let me give you an example of what God's life can do. A young lady who had three cancerous tumors in her uterus recently came into my office. When she walked in, the first thing I said to her was, "Do you realize what you just did?" I stared at her; I wanted to make her uncomfortable.

She said, "I just walked into your office."

I said, "That's right. Do you know what that means?"

"No."

I said, "I don't have cancer in my room. I don't believe in it. If you walk in my office, you submit to the life of God within me and cancer will die."

I asked her, "Are you ready to get healed?"

She said, "Yes."

I asked her to have a seat, and I began to minister to her for awhile about the life of God, about not giving up, about the fact that it was not as it seemed, that God's power was in there doing a work inside of her.

The next week, she went back to the doctor. After viewing her, the doctor said, "Well, I'm sorry to say these three tumors have gotten larger. I've already ordered your radiation treatment; you're going to have to start immediately."

She said, "I'm sorry to say this, too, doctor, but I don't believe that."

Her doctor said, "What do you mean you don't believe it? I've got proof right here: Look."

She said, "I'm sorry, I don't need to look. I don't believe it. It can't be that way, because I know that Jesus has healed me. I know that my body's not that way."

He said, "Well, I've got proof to say that it is."

She said, "Well, I've got proof to say that it isn't."

The doctor said, "I'm going to bring in another doctor to let him try to argue with you."

Another doctor came in, and she said the same thing to him.

He said, "Well, young lady, just to prove to you that you have three tumors, we'll take another ultrasound."

So they took another ultrasound, and the doctor explained that it looked as if a laser had been used to cut out one of those tumors. The tumor appeared to have been hit by something because it had broken up into a bunch of small pieces and had come away from her body.

They'd never seen anything like this before. They said that normally when this happens, those pieces will go all through the body and spread. In other words, if they took a laser and hit that tumor, they could break that tumor up, but then it would begin to spread.

They said there were two unusual things about this.

First, when a laser goes to sever something, it always leaves scar tissue; they could find none. It was as though it had never existed in her body.

Second, once that thing broke into small pieces, one way or another there was a sack that encompassed them and did not allow them to go anywhere.

Doctors said, "We've never seen anything like this before. However, we still need to do radiation."

She said, "No, you don't, because I'm the healed of the Lord."

They brought in another doctor to look at it. He said, "Well, I've got to go in there and see this for myself."

He went in there with a third ultrasound. The same thing had happened to the second tumor. There it was, broken up into many different pieces encompassed in a sack so those pieces could not spread around.

> *The Word of God is alive and powerful and sharper than any two-edged sword.*

At that point, several doctors were in that room viewing this, saying they had never before seen anything like it.

Then they said, "We've got to go back in there to see what's happening to the third one."

They went back and looked at the third one, and it had diminished to half the size.

Now they said, "Instead of radiation, ma'am, what would you like to do about the third one?"

She said, "Well, I'll come back in a week, and you'll see that it's gone."

Praise the Lord, two weeks later, it was gone, just as she had said.

Hebrews 4:12 says that the Word of God is alive and powerful and sharper than any two-edged sword. That sword cut out all those growths, and it can do the same for you. The anointing of God, which destroyed those tumors, is in the room with you now. You don't *have* to feel it, but you *can* feel it. While you're reading these pages, the power of God is working. Remember, the Word of God is the *power* of God.

You just have to believe in it, just as this woman believed that tumors could not enter my office. If we understand that the life of God is within us, God will perform a miracle every time.

A MIRACLE EVERY TIME

I have witnessed this principle in action many times. For example, once I laid hands on a lady and prayed for her jaw, which had been out of place and not even surgery could repair it. The next morning, when she went back for a checkup, her specialist said, "This is a miracle. I don't know how this happened, but your jaw is perfectly aligned.

Whether God shaved or shrunk some bone—whatever He did—He put it back in place."

Another time a man who had been injured in an accident asked me to pray for his leg. A steel plate had been fastened with four screws to his shin, and that leg was two inches shorter than the other.

I told him, "That's nothing for God. He'll either grow bone out or grow metal out—one or the other—but your leg is coming out."

That leg grew out one inch the first night after I agreed with him in prayer. And the next morning it grew out the other inch. That is extraordinary! That is *super*natural!

A man came to the Healing Center to be ministered to for cancer in his brain. The doctors had given him up to die. A team of our healing workers began to minister the Word to him. Throughout the week his faith was strengthened. At the end of the week the workers and I again instructed him concerning the faith that he had *in* him and how impossible it would be for it *not* to work a miracle. We laid hands on him and began to pray in the Holy Spirit.

Shortly thereafter, he came back to the Center to tell us that his doctor confirmed that he is completely healed of cancer. He explained to us that on the day we laid hands on him and prayed in the Holy Spirit, the sound he heard was to him the same as the sound made by the radiation machines used in his treatments.

He went on to say that where my hands touched his head, he had the sensation or awareness that something was being extracted from his head. As confirmed by examination, evidently this is exactly what God did because the doctor verified that the tumor had disappeared with no trace or sign of cancer remaining. Praise the Lord! We have the life of God in abundance dwelling in our beings.

God Almighty lives inside of you. Did you lock Him up inside and throw away the key? You may not think so, but if you think of yourself as a poor old beggar just trying to barely get along, hoping that somehow or another your doctors will come up with a new drug to cure your illness, or you'll win the lottery before going bankrupt, then I'm telling you right now, your conscience has locked God up, and He is useless to you. The lack of Godly recognition will alienate you from God's ability. (Eph. 4:18.)

> *Hold on to who you are in Christ.*

It's as though you put a $100 bill in that secret place in your billfold but forgot it was there. And when you are short on gas money, you have to call someone to help you pay for a fill-up. And all the while you have a $100 bill in your pocket. It's there, but you don't use it. It is useless to you because of your ignorance.

Paul said, "Come on! Do you want to be a prizefighter? I don't beat the air. If I swing, I hit my target. Do you want to be a fighter and hit your target? I will tell you how to fight in faith: Hold on to who you are in Christ; hold on to eternal life." (1 Tim. 6:12; 1 Cor. 9:26.)

Eternal life is the quality of the kind of life that we now have as God's children. We don't have to wait until we get to eternity to grasp eternal life. We are eternal beings now, and the Bible says that the eternal quality of Almighty God has come inside of us in exchange for that deadly, doomed quality that we had through sin, sickness, and disease.

Now eternal life is inside us. We did not do anything to merit the ability of God, but thank God we are well-schooled about *what* we have and *whom* we have. We can proclaim, "Jesus is inside of me!"

A STEP UP

What it means to have Christ inside us is that our lives are stepped up, increased both in quality and quantity. Our life source comes from a different place. We have a new Daddy. We are *sons* of God! We are made of a new substance. We may look like the same person we were before Jesus gave us His life, but glory to God, on the inside we are nothing like we used to be!

It wouldn't surprise me one bit if, as you read about this, you just jumped up completely whole and strong in Jesus' name. There's enough power inside of you to blow up every kind of cancer and every HIV strain a million times over. There's enough power inside of you to bring a miracle into your home, your job, your friendships—every part of your life—right now.

Proverbs 23:7 says that as a man thinks in his heart, so is he. When we begin to see some of the truths of who we really are in Christ, all of a sudden we will realize the truth that "greater is He who is in us than he who is in the world." (1 John 4:4.) Nothing will ever overcome us, for we walk and live by the faith of a Champion.

Chapter Ten

Accept Your Role as Qualified

❧

G od successfully established a way to assist and bless fallen man. Ultimately, the fullness of this plan would bring Jesus on the scene to alter and reestablish the pure heart of God. Though one man caused death to spread to all, one man also provided righteousness to all. The first man, Adam,

> *Every human being is created a spirit being in God's likeness.*

brought sin and its consciousness to humanity; the second man, Jesus, brought life and it's consciousness into the world. The road to obtain life is faith.

Every human being is created a spirit being in God's likeness. We are capable of receiving and arranging information as well as believing and processing that information.

God intended for faith and the miraculous to be the very core of man's existence.

In a sinful condition, man has chosen to except the low road, processing and creating human ideas according to his own ability. It takes faith operating in the heart of man to develop and create the highest thoughts—God's thoughts. We are the sum total of our thoughts and aspirations.

God began with a man named Abram to produce the highest type of belief known to this earth—God's faith! Within the framework of a blood covenant, God successfully satisfied Abram's soul through liberty to express his trust and reliance on God's Word. The result was the *impossible!*

Throughout the Bible, history records the supernatural as common place. Why has the supernatural become so uncommon in our day? Could it be that our generation has left our first love and lost sight of the importance of covenant? We subconsciously water down the doctrine of faith in exchange for a doctrine of works. We have learned to cope with our difficulties because the frustration of failure seems unbearable. This was never God's plan.

God intended for faith and the miraculous to be the very core of man's existence. Jesus conquered the devil, the source of our difficulty, and restored man to the dominion of authority. Sometimes it doesn't appear as if Jesus succeeded. After all, the devil, sickness, and disease have been defeated and are no longer in control. Man should have very little trouble with the devil unless he is unaware of his seat of authority and his triumphant victory through his place in Christ.

We must contend earnestly for the faith that was once given. (Jude 3.) The devil desires to divert our attention from the work Christ finished. Perhaps we struggle with leaving our work ethic to gain acceptance. We don't have to do anything to merit God's approval.

Favor is something inherited; not worked for. He has given us everything necessary to enforce Christ's victory every time, all the time. God has provided the means to live without sin, sickness, disease, poverty, and the oppressions of the defeated devil and his assistants. Let's use our faith to reveal God's plan.

Knowing that you have faith is a position of confidence and a great place to begin. Too much time is wasted *working* to obtain faith when it already exists within the heart of the believer. Since the believer must have a steadfast, immovable demeanor to accompany his faith, know you have what it takes to win. Confidence is essential for victory.

Enough cannot be said for the heart of a champion who will not accept defeat. Look at what Paul said in 2 Corinthians 4:13, "For we, having the same spirit of faith." What does Paul mean by the phrase "spirit of faith"? Elsewhere when Paul writes using the phrase "spirit of" as in Ephesians 4:23, "And be renewed in the spirit of your mind," he is concerned with the attitude of your mind.

Let's look briefly at the life of the apostle Paul and see what he means. First, he received his doctrine directly from the Lord Jesus Christ.

But I certify you, brethren, that the gospel which was preached of me is not after man. For I neither received it of man, neither was I taught it, but by the revelation of Jesus Christ. For ye have heard of my conversation in time past in the Jews' religion, how that beyond measure I persecuted the church of God, and wasted it: And profited in the Jews' religion above many my equals in mine own nation, being more exceedingly zealous of the traditions of my fathers. But when it pleased God, who separated me from my mother's womb, and called me by his grace, to reveal his Son in me, that I might preach him among the heathen;

> *Paul caught the spirit of Christ's triumph.*

immediately I conferred not with flesh and blood (Gal 1:11-16).

Can you imagine being a zealot, bound to every letter of the law, radical concerning your views, and then Jesus reveals Himself to you? Jesus shared with Paul that he was a *champion* filled with power and authority. He revealed the mystery of redemption, Christ in you, the hope of Glory. He shared His heart and love concerning the world, and throughout this revelation Paul gained insight into the spirit or attitude that made Jesus victorious. He wrote in Hebrews 12:2, "Looking unto Jesus the author and finisher of our faith; who for the joy that was set before him endured the cross, despising the shame, and is set down at the right hand of the throne of God."

He grasped the heart of the undefeated Lord, who with His eye on the victory could face death with a joyful heart and in view of the glorious triumph despise temporary discomfort. Paul caught the spirit of Christ's triumph.

For example, consider the apostles receiving the commission to heal the sick and cast out devils. Paul continually worked the miraculous without failure; the transmission of information and inspiration was at an all time peak level.

When we have a great need, we go to a specialist for advice. Their expertise assures us of something we don't possess; the mastery of the situation. When they convey information to us they give us more than their professional opinion; they transmit their spirit and demeanor of success.

With this in mind, can you see Jesus declaring to the disciples that all authority has been given to me in heaven and earth, therefore, go and preach the gospel? When something is so real to you and fresh to your memory, it is understood that you will receive and embrace it as more than information.

Paul definitely captured the heart of the Lord.

We are troubled on every side, yet not distressed; we are perplexed, but not in despair; persecuted, but not forsaken; cast down, but not destroyed; always bearing about in the body the dying of the Lord

Jesus, that the life also of Jesus might be made manifest in our body. For we which live are always delivered unto death for Jesus' sake, that the life also of Jesus might be made manifest in our mortal flesh. So then death worketh in us, but life in you. We having the same spirit of faith, according as it is written, I believed, and therefore have I spoken; we also believe, and therefore speak (2 Corinthians 4:8-13).

> *There is no time to question your faith in the midst of adversity; we must remain steadfast, being reminded of what we believe.*

We can see the commitment of Paul. He really believed in the work of God. Throughout all the stressful situations, Paul maintained the steadfastness to be immovable and always abound. His encouragement to the churches contained one of the greatest revelations Paul received, "My grace is sufficient for you, in your weakness I will make you strong" (2 Cor. 12:9).

This is the position of the believer. There is no time to question your faith in the midst of adversity; we must remain steadfast, being reminded of what we believe. Perhaps this is the reason that Paul spent so much time admonishing and encouraging the church.

Therefore, when we could no longer endure it, we thought it good to be left in Athens alone, and sent Timothy, our brother and minister of God, and our fellow laborer in the gospel of Christ, to establish you and encourage you concerning your faith, that no one should be shaken by these afflictions; for you yourselves know that we are

> *Looking at the Word is like beholding your reflection in a mirror.*

appointed to this. For, in fact, we told you before when we were with you that we would suffer tribulation, just as it happened, and you know. For this reason, when I could no longer endure it, I sent to know your faith, lest by some means the tempter had tempted you, and our labor might be in vain" (1 Thessalonians 3:1-5).

The only thing that would cause their labor to be in vain would be to retreat from the place of victory. Establishing and encouraging one's faith is the glue that bonds your actions and victory together. Just like the time Jesus encouraged Jairus not to fear, but to believe. Jairus continued to believe and his action kept the victory in the hands of Jesus. James admonished us that faith without works is dead. Hearing the Word alone will not make you act on it. Yet it will encourage you to act the more you renew your thoughts to the thoughts of God.

Looking at the Word is like beholding your reflection in a mirror. The longer you see yourself qualified for a miracle, the more likely you will receive one. James said that if you don't act on the Word, although you are listening to it, you will deceive yourself.

GO TO THE SCRIPT

If I were considering an acting career, I would look for opportunities to audition for a part in a movie. Before I could audition I would review a script of the character I want to portray. Knowing the script ensures the success of my audition. It contains the words I need to memorize for my lines. However, it contains much more than words. It provides the setting and mood of the movie.

> *Everything we need to manifest God's nature is found in the script.*

Words are lifeless without understanding the setting and the mood. There are many ways a word can be said and an action given.

If you were cast as the hero, you should respond as a hero. Even if you didn't *feel* like a hero, you must act like one to master the part. Your success depends on your ability to act. Are you able to adopt the attitude and mentality of the character portrayed?

When the director says, "action," you become the film's hero, relinquishing your own identity. While the film rolls, you immerse body and soul into the role. To play the part, you must meet the script demands.

The same principle should be applied in learning to use God's faith. The ability to walk in God's nature—His love, joy, peace, longsuffering, gentleness, goodness, faith, meekness, and self-control—is limited by our knowledge. That is why it's important to renew our minds to the Word of God. The Bible is our script to show us how a qualified believer acts.

The Scriptures are a script we portray in life on earth. Life will challenge us with many events and experiences that oppose the script, but we must learn how to take our script and act out the truth.

For example, life might try to tell you that you have cancer in your body and you are not going to make it. You need to say, "Jesus took my diseases. (Isa. 53:5; 1 Peter 2:24.) If He took my cancer, what am I doing with it?"

Everything we need to manifest God's nature is found in the script. When a certain situation comes up, and we do not know how to respond in faith, we must simply look in the script at the different illustrations of individuals who exercised their faith.

In Luke 8:44, we look at the woman who kept pressing to Jesus until she touched the hem of His garment and was healed. Then we say,

"Faith doesn't back up; faith always goes forward. That is what faith looks like, so that is what I look like."

In Joshua 6:2-20, we look at the children of Israel marching around Jericho and shouting, "Glory! Glory! Glory!" until the seventh time when the walls came down. We can take that demeanor and act it out. Begin to shout before we see our results. That is what faith does.

We read the script, not so we can "get some more faith," but so we can portray who we really are—new creatures filled with the Spirit of God and all *His* attributes.

When we look into God's Word, we see the very picture of who we really are. Remember when you believed in Jesus, you became something you weren't before. You became a new creature, a believer. You became a Christian. Regardless of how you feel, you are a qualified believer made in the image of the greatest champion of all times—Jesus.

As a child of God, we are to live life on a different plane, a new level of existence. We study the script to reveal *who we are in Christ*. Everything we see in the Word that reflects the image of Christ is exactly who we are.

Think of the limitless possibilities! The similarities of the actor and actress to the Christian are the actions, the words, and the attitudes portrayed.

Truly, as our Father directs this film, the Holy Spirit as our Coach helps us portray the prototype of Jesus. Webster's defines *prototype* as an original model on which something is patterned.[1] I cannot think of a better place to be encouraged, than to know that my being has been made a *faith being* with the faith of God for eternal success. My heart leaps with joy concerning my future! My success as a Christian is secure. I am qualified and the victory has been won! Is it any wonder that Jesus said, *"all things are possible to him who believes"*?

SECRETS TO RECEIVING FROM GOD

God made it simple for Abram to act on His Word.

❧

God's objective is to bless all who believe Him.

❧

God viewed Abram's question as worthy of an answer.

❧

*In order for God to cut a covenant He had to find someone
equal to or greater than Himself.*

❧

*The natural things that God did on Abram's level helped him
trust and instantly believe what God said.*

❧

Jesus became as we are, so that we could become as He is.

❧

*God's ultimate goal for Abraham, and indeed all of
humankind, was to get him to believe.*

❧

God calls people who are born again "righteousness."

❧

Just as brides traditionally take on the names of their husbands, when we become Christians we take on the name of Christ.

❧

Doubt is unnatural.

❧

Anything God promises will be easy for us to believe and receive.

❧

Two areas of your life that a sin nature affects are your flesh and your mind.

❧

We are God's product, God's display, and God's work of art.

❧

In order to preserve our spirits when His holy presence came inside, God lined our spirits with Himself.

❧

We're not trying to become like Jesus; we already are like Jesus!

❧

You're not just natural anymore; you're supernatural.

❧

I've made you a whole new being that looks and acts just like Me!

❧

A Christian declares what is according to My Word, and then he watches it take place exactly as I said it.

We must accept God's gift of righteousness.

God's belief is God's faith.

It doesn't come if you don't express what you believe.

We can only receive God results with God's faith.

*Continuing to hear the word will water the seed and fortify
your effectviveness as a doer of the Word.*

*We must completely depend upon God's Word, or God's faith,
to follow in Jesus' footsteps.*

*We are responsible for the stewardship of
our faith toward God.*

*Grace is God's ability to do for you what you
can't do for yourself.*

*When you act on the belief that comes from God, then it also
includes His ability and faithfulness to bring it to pass.*

*It's not the proportion of the faith that you possess;
it's the proportion you use.*

When we became one with God — so much so that
all of our liabilities became His, and all of
His assets become ours.

∽◈∽

His peace came into our spirits in a
more-than-enough measure.

∽◈∽

God placed all of His nature inside of us when we received
His gift of salvation.

∽◈∽

We need to understand that God's attributes are ours, and
therefore, we cannot fail.

∽◈∽

Why don't you use your faith?

∽◈∽

The greatness of his faith was the way he used what he heard.

∽◈∽

It is not in our own ability to make our faith big enough to
meet the task.

∽◈∽

The greatness of her belief was in her determination
not to give up.

∽◈∽

If we are "in the faith," we have come out of this world and
have been translated into another world.

∽◈∽

The way people think about themselves will determine the way they use their faith.

❧

Our frame of mind affects the outcome of everything we do.

❧

There is no compromise in the voice of a believer who absolutely believes what God said.

❧

The battle is not about getting some faith; it's about conquering doubt so you can use God's faith effectively.

❧

You can't fail using God's faith.

❧

When you know it's God's faith working in you, you won't let up.

❧

By our attitudes, we create the environment around ourselves.

❧

Pride put Satan in a position to fall.

❧

The only cure for mortality is immortality.

❧

The Word of God is alive and powerful and sharper than any two-edged sword.

❧

Hold on to who you are in Christ.

❧

Every human being is created a spirit being in God's likeness.

❧

*God intended for faith and the miraculous to be
the very core of man's existence.*

❧

Paul caught the spirit of Christ's triumph.

❧

*There is no time to question your faith in the midst of
adversity; we must remain steadfast, being reminded
of what we believe.*

❧

*Looking at the Word is like beholding your
reflection in a mirror.*

❧

*Everything we need to manifest God's nature is
found in the script.*

❧

ENDNOTES

Foreword

[1] Way, Arthur S.

Chapter 4

[1] Strong, "Greek," #5083.

[2] *The Bible in Basic English.*

[3] Strong, "Greek," #4957.

[4] Strong, "Greek," #4916.

Chapter 5

[1] Willmington, Dr. H. L.

[2] Ibid.

Chapter 6

[1] *Webster's Ninth New Collegiate Dictionary,* p. 788, s.v. "natural."

[2] *Webster's Ninth New Collegiate Dictionary,* p. 789, s.v. "nature."

[3] s.v. *workmanship.*

[4] s.v. *create.*

[5] s.v. *Christ* Merrill F. Unger & R. K. Harrison.

Chapter 9

1 Strongs, "Greek" #2222 "zoe."

2 Ibid.

Chapter 10

1 *Webster's Ninth New Collegiate Dictionary*, p. 491, s.v. "prototype."

REFERENCES

Merrill F. Unger & R. K. Harrison, *The New Unger's Bible Dictionary;* Chicago, Illinois: Moody Press, 1988, "Christ".

Strong, James. *Strong's Exhaustive Concordance of the Bible.* "Greek Dictionary of the New Testament." Nashville: Abingdon, 1890.

Webster's Ninth New Collegiate Dictionary, Merriam-Webster Inc., Publishers; Springfield, Massachusetts, U.S.A. Copyright 1988 by Merriam-Webster.

Way, Arthur S., *The Letters of St. Paul to the Seven Churches and Three Friends with the Letter to the Hebrews.* Sixth Edition. Mac Million and Company, New York, New York, 1926.

Willmington, Dr. H. L. *Wilmington's Guide to the Bible.* Tyndale House Publishers, Inc., Wheaton, Illinois: 1981, 1st printing, page 451.

ABOUT THE AUTHOR

Jim Hockaday was born again at four years of age. Experiencing the call of God at this time and the desire to preach, Jim led many to the Lord during his childhood. After graduation from Wheaton College in 1983, he traveled with various musical groups including Spurlows, Truth, and Living Word Singers.

Jim attended Rhema Bible Training Center and graduated in 1988. Immediately following graduation he joined the *Rhema Singers and Band* and traveled extensively with Rev. Kenneth E. Hagin for nearly seven years; during the last several years he had the management responsibility of the Group. Jim was the coordinator of Prayer and Healing School for Kenneth Hagin Ministries, completing his tenth year in May 2004. He founded *Jim Hockaday Ministries, Inc.* in 1991, and now travels and ministers full time in churches at home and abroad.

Jim is the author of several books, one of which is the best selling book, "Until I Come"... and the most recent release, *"Where Does God Fit In?"*

Jim, his wife Erin (a 1991 graduate of Rhema Bible Training Center and member of The Rhema Singers and Band for two and a half years), and daughters Alli, Drew, and Chloe reside in the Tulsa area.

To contact the author please write:

Jim Hockaday Ministries, Inc.

P.O. Box 839

Broken Arrow, OK 74013

We welcome your comments,
prayer requests, and
especially your miracles!

PRAYER OF SALVATION

A born-again, committed relationship with God is the key to a victorious life. Jesus, the Son of God, laid down His life and rose again so that we could spend eternity with Him in heaven and experience His absolute best on earth. The Bible says, "For God so loved the world, that he gave his only begotten Son, that whosoever believeth in him should not perish, but have everlasting life" (John 3:16).

It is the will of God that everyone receives eternal salvation. The way to receive this salvation is to call upon the name of Jesus and confess Him as your Lord. The Bible says, "That if thou shalt confess with thy mouth the Lord Jesus, and shalt believe in thine heart that God hath raised him from the dead, thou shalt be saved. For whosoever shall call upon the name of the Lord shall be saved" (Romans 10:9-10,13).

Jesus has given salvation, healing, and countless benefits to all who call upon His name. These benefits can be yours if you receive Him into your heart by praying this prayer:

Heavenly Father, I come to You admitting that I am a sinner. Right now, I choose to turn away from sin, and I ask You to cleanse me of all unrighteousness. I believe that Your Son, Jesus, died on the cross to take away my sins. I also believe that He rose again from the dead so that I may be justified and made righteous through faith in Him. I call upon the name of Jesus

Christ to be the Savior and Lord of my life. Jesus, I choose to follow You, and I ask that You fill me with the power of the Holy Spirit. I declare right now that I am a born-again child of God. I am free from sin, and full of the righteousness of God. I am saved in Jesus' name, Amen.

If you have prayed this prayer to receive Jesus Christ as your Savior, or if this book has changed your life, we would like to hear from you. Please write us at:

Jim Hockaday Ministries, Inc.
P.O. Box 839
Broken Arrow, OK 74013